EXCEL 2021

THE COMPLETE BEGINNER TO EXPERT GUIDE

Master the Essential Functions and Formulas in Less Than 10 Minutes per Day With Step-by-Step Tutorials and Practical Examples

Anthony Python

TABLE OF CONTENTS

INTRODUCTION

Microsoft Excel is a spreadsheet program, sometimes known as a workbook. A workbook is a computer program that lets you enter a sequence of numbers and other information. The Excel application's goal is to allow users to collect similar data in one place for present and future usage.

Microsoft Excel is one of several spreadsheet programs available. Before the debut of Excel w, Lotus 123 was one of the most popular spreadsheets in the 1980s. Excel was released in 1984-1985. It was created for the Apple Macintosh computer system.

Other spreadsheet applications exist and have existed in the past, but Excel and Lotus are the most frequently used. Nearly every company in the United States, if not the whole world, uses Microsoft Excel. Alternatively, for IBM compatible PCs or Apple systems. Spreadsheets have become so popular that my daughter learned how to use them in fifth grade. This indicates that Microsoft Excel will continue to be used for years, if not decades, to come as long as Microsoft continues to improve the product and remain ahead of the competition.

Do you work with Excel? If so, when did you first hear about it? Do you prefer Excel on a PC or an Apple device? Do you utilize Excel Macros (VBA) as well? The backbone of Microsoft Excel is macros, which are built up of VBA. Users can utilize it to automate parts of their work. If you often copy and paste data from one sheet to another, you may construct a macro to automate the process, saving you time in the future. You may either record the Excel macro or input the Excel VBA that creates it. The simplest method to begin automating your files is to record Excel macros.

The code that creates the macro may then be viewed in the VBA editor. You can edit your macro by changing one or more lines of code. The more you do it, the more you will learn. Before you know it, you'll be an expert. It only takes some time and effort. Anyone can learn Excel VBA because there are so many good books on the subject. Google is another excellent resource. Type in Excel VBA. Help to uncover a plethora of learning materials, most of which are free.

You may also hire an Excel VBA specialist to assist you with your documents. While this is more expensive, it allows you to receive findings much more quickly, typically within hours or the same day. If you're not sure where to seek an excel expert, type "excel experts" into Google, and you'll get many results. Look through the first five Google results to see if any excel consulting companies show up. Take a look at the website if that's the case. Please remember that you'll need more than an excel expert; you'll need an excel expert who also understands how to use Excel VBA. Many of them don't, so you may have to search for one that does.

If you're using Excel on a Mac, consider that VBA is only accessible in a few versions.

1. WHAT IS EXCEL AND THINGS YOU CAN MAKE WITH IT

Microsoft has announced two new Office versions: Office 2021 for consumers and Office LTSC for commercial clients. It is intended for people who do not wish to subscribe to the cloud-powered Microsoft 365 versions, as was the prior Office 2019 edition.

Microsoft has not yet completely detailed all of the features and improvements in Office 2021. Nonetheless, the Office LTSC (Long-Term Servicing Channel) edition will contain dark mode support, accessibility enhancements, and Excel capabilities such as Dynamic Arrays and XLOOKUP. Similar features will be included in Office 2021. There will be no substantial UI changes here, either. The dark mode is a visible shift, but Microsoft will continue to prioritize the UI and cloud-powered features in the Microsoft 365 editions of Office.

However, Office LTSC is a clear indication from Microsoft that not all of its corporate customers are ready to migrate to the cloud. "It's a question of trying to meet consumers where they are," says Jared Spataro, Microsoft

365 chief, in an interview with The Verge. "We certainly have a lot of clients who have gone to the cloud in the last ten months; that has happened in a big way. Simultaneously, we have clients that have particular circumstances in which they do not believe they can migrate to the cloud."

THIS UPCOMING OFFICE RELEASE IS FOR THOSE WHO DO NOT WISH TO USE MICROSOFT 365.

These examples include regulated businesses where processes and programs cannot be changed every month and industrial factories that rely on Office and require a fixed time release. Microsoft is also committed to another permanent edition of Office in the future, but the cost and support for these new versions are changing. Office LTSC will now be supported for five years rather than the seven years that Microsoft has traditionally guaranteed for Office. Office Professional Plus, Office Standard, and individual licenses are all priced differently. Applications are also increasing by 10% for commercial users, but consumer and small business pricing for Office 2021 remains unchanged.

The timing of Office LTSC support is more closely aligned with how Windows is supported. Microsoft is likewise tightening the gap between its Office and Windows release timetables. In the second half of 2021, the next editions of Office LTSC and Windows 10 LTSC will be launched. "They will be tightly timed," adds Spataro, "although we do not yet have the details for the Windows release." "The goal is to bring them together so that companies can deploy and manage them on the same cadence."

Microsoft aims to deliver an Office LTSC preview in April, followed by a complete release later. However, the consumer Office 2021 edition will not be accessible in preview. Both of the new Office editions will feature OneNote and will be available in 32-bit and 64-bit versions. When I tell folks about the many data analysis applications I use, I occasionally receive blank looks when I mention MS Excel. Many people forget that not everyone is familiar with Microsoft Excel and its features. Microsoft Excel, or simply Excel, is an electronic spreadsheet application commonly used to store data. After you've saved your data, you may utilize MS Excel to organize and edit it. It's critical to arrange data in a meaningful way to make manipulating it to discover answers or patterns easier.

When you launch Microsoft Excel 2013, it appears to be identical to MS Excel 2007 and 2010. The interface will change if you're using an earlier version of Excel, but the concept of a spreadsheet will stay the same.

So, when I open Excel, what do I see?

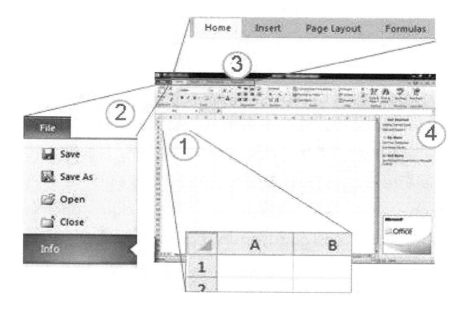

When you start Excel 2007 or later, you'll see a ribbon of commands that will assist you in performing any tasks you need to do fast. A rectangular table, sometimes known as a grid, with rows and columns is located beneath the ribbon. The numbers in the left column on the left side of the screen identify the rows. An Excel spreadsheet may have up to 1,048,576 rows. The columns are labeled with letters ranging from A to Z at the top of the table, followed by two or more letters, for a total of 16,384 columns. Even though you have all of these rows and columns at your disposal, keep in mind that the more information you include, the lower the quality of your spreadsheet will be since the capability of your computer restricts you.

The first cell where you can enter data is labeled A1, indicating that it is located in column A, row 1. A cell reference is another name for this.

It's worth noting that the first column A and the first row 1 are both dark green. That's how you find out what each cell's cell reference or address is.

What kinds of data can you store in a cell?

Numbers, text, links, and formulae are examples of data types that may be stored in a cell. Excel includes a comprehensive collection of formulae that you may use to alter your data. The formulae are located on the ribbon under the Formulas tab in MS Excel 2007 and subsequent versions. Excel's strength rests in its ability to manipulate data.

What are the Benefits of MS Excel?

Excel may be used for a variety of tasks. Some of the things you can accomplish are as follows:

• Basic mathematical calculations such as sum, product, min, max, average.

• Manipulate financial data to calculate profit or loss

• Figure out repayment plans for different rates on loans and mortgages

• Build a personal/family budget

• Graph data in charts

• Pivot Tables and charts to sort and filter data

• Write small apps called macros to automate daily tasks

How can I use MS Excel data for my presentation needs?

I usually use Excel to manipulate data and find patterns. When I'm happy with the information I've gathered and modified, I can typically copy it and paste it wherever I want, for example:

• Other MS Excel Workbooks

• MS Word file

• Web Pages - I first save it as an image

• Presentations - PowerPoint easily accepts tables and charts from Excel. Just copy from Excel and paste directly to the presentations. I usually select to paste as a picture, but it can also be useful to leave the table/chart as a functioning table/chart for easy manipulation within PowerPoint.

• Print - Printing is an easy way to distribute information from Excel.

MS Excel is used for storing data, analyzing and sorting data, and reporting on a basic level. Spreadsheets are immensely popular in business since they are highly visual and relatively simple to use.

Business analysis, human resource management, performance reporting, and operations management are some of the most popular business uses of MS Excel. After reviewing job data, we can confidently say that this is true (using MS Excel).

1. Business Analysis

Business analysis is the most common application of MS Excel in the workplace.

Business analysis is the process of using data to help people make better decisions. Businesses naturally collect data in their day-to-day operations, such as product sales, website traffic, supply expenditures, insurance claims, and so on.

Turning data into something usable for the people who manage the firm is known as business analysis. You might, for example, generate a profit report based on the day of the week.

2. People Management

You might be shocked to find that one of the most common uses of Excel in the workplace is to manage people.

MS Excel is a wonderful tool for organizing data about individuals, whether they are workers, clients, sponsors, or attendees at a training session.

Personal information may be effectively saved and accessed using Excel. An individual record can be stored in a spreadsheet row or column with name, email address, employee start date, products purchased, subscription status, and last contact.

3. Managing Operations

Many organizations rely significantly on Excel to run their day-to-day operations.

When it comes to business, logistics may be extremely difficult. Inventory flows must be managed to keep operations operating smoothly – and to avoid overstocking on specific goods. This includes keeping track of supplier and customer transactions, organizing a calendar of important events, and managing time and schedules.

While Amazon's operations are managed using sophisticated proprietary software, MS Excel is a vital tool for many small enterprises (or parts of larger businesses). Excel has the benefit of being relatively low-tech, allowing it to be utilized by many individuals without the danger of programming problems.

4. Performance Reporting

Performance monitoring and reporting is a sort of business analysis that may be accomplished with MS Excel. Many accountants, for example, continue to use Excel (in part because it is compatible with cloud-based accounting software).

A pivot table is a typical technique to transform data into a performance report in Excel. You may easily add relevant information to a dataset by introducing a pivot table and tying it to data. Pivot tables come with several built-in functions that allow you to do activities like counting and summing specific categories of data inside a dataset.

5. Office Administration

Much of the data needed for accounting and financial reporting and business analysis and performance reporting are entered and stored in Excel by office administrators.

Excel is important in office administration for assisting day-to-day operations like invoicing, paying bills, contacting suppliers and clients, and recordkeeping. It's a multi-functional application for tracking and organizing workplace operations.

Administrative assistant, administration officer, administration supervisor, administrative assistant, business operations and office manager, junior clerical and administrative officer, office admin manager, office support – maintenance / general tasks are just a few examples of job titles.

6. Strategic Analysis

Strategic analysis is a type of Excel analysis in which business choices are tightly linked to data and formulae on spreadsheets. You use Excel to help you make decisions about investments and asset allocations.

For example, you could opt to get currency insurance based on an Excel model. Spreadsheet analysis is intended to help you make particular business decisions.

7. Project Management

Even though project managers have access to purpose-built project management (PM) software, an Excel Workbook is frequently a viable option.

Projects are a type of commercial activity that has a budget and a start and finish date. Project plans may be entered into a workbook, which can be used to track progress and stay on track.

One benefit of utilizing Excel is sharing the project worksheet with others, even if they are unfamiliar with or don't have access to bespoke PM software.

8. Program Management

Excel is an excellent program management tool. It may be customized to handle the unique characteristics of particular software. Because MS Excel is widely used, numerous persons may readily handle program records and pass them over to a new manager when the time comes.

A program is similar to a project, except it can be ongoing and reliant on user engagement. Managers can use MS Excel to allocate resources, track progress, and keep track of participant information.

9. Contract Administration

MS Excel is popular among contract administrators because it makes it simple to keep track of contract data such as dates, milestones, deliverables, and payments.

There are several contract management templates to choose from, each of which may be customized to fit the contract type or stage of the contract lifecycle.

10. Account Management

Because they receive and must keep client records, account managers are typically expected to be proficient MS Excel users.

An account manager must maintain ties with the company's current customers. Customer loyalty and repeat sales are important objectives. It's a marketing-oriented position that's a popular choice among MBA grads.

Excel is often used in account management since it makes sharing and maintaining customer files straightforward.

2. GETTING STARTED WITH MS EXCEL

E xcel is a spreadsheet application that allows you to organize, store, and analyze data. While you may believe that only specific people use Excel to analyze complex data, anybody can learn how to use the program's sophisticated capabilities. Excel makes it simple to deal with many sorts of data, whether you're managing a budget, compiling a training log, or producing an invoice.

We'll also cover how to insert data into cells, copy and transfer data, and propagate cell contents, among other things. We'll walk you through every step of learning all you need to know about Microsoft Excel. We recommend that you open Excel and use the steps below to create your spreadsheet.

Using Microsoft Excel, you may create spreadsheets by arranging rows and columns in a table. Data may be kept in the worksheet as a Microsoft Word table, also known as a spreadsheet. Still, Excel's strength lies in its capacity to do simple to sophisticated mathematical calculations and other tasks. See Excel Math Basics when you're ready to construct some math formulae.

The Worksheet (Spreadsheet) and Workbook in Excel

A spreadsheet, often known as an Excel worksheet, is a two-dimensional grid containing columns and rows. Take a look at the spreadsheet that follows. The columns are named after letters of the alphabet beginning with A, while the rows are numbered sequentially, beginning with one. A1, B1, C1, and so on are the first row's cells. A1, A2, A3, and so on are the cells in the first column. Cell names or cell references are what they're termed.

When writing arithmetic formulae or functions, we utilize cell references. To combine the contents of cells B2 and B3, for example, use the formula =B2+B3.

The Name Box, which is above Column A, displays the cell reference of the selected cell - the cell where the cursor is now positioned. C2 is the chosen cell in our spreadsheet. The color of the column letter (C) and the row number (2) both change.

On our worksheet, the beginning of the Formula Bar can be seen above Column D. The contents of the chosen cell are displayed in the Formula Bar.

A collection of worksheets or spreadsheets is referred to as a workbook. When you launch Excel, it creates a workbook with three blank worksheets. The names of the worksheets are shown in the Excel window on tabs at the bottom of the window.

How to Get From One Cell to Another

Use the arrow keys to navigate left, right, up, and down from the current cell. To shift one cell to the right, use the Tab key and enter to go directly below the current cell.

How to Choose Cells

In an Excel spreadsheet, you may select cells in a variety of ways:

• Click within a cell to choose it.

• Click on the row number to choose one or more rows of cells (s).

• Click on the column letter to choose one or more columns of cells (s).

• Click on one corner cell and drag the mouse to the other corner to pick a set of adjacent cells. We've picked cells A1 through B5 in the picture on the right (written A1:B5 in formulas).

• When you click on the relevant cells, hold down the Ctrl key as you click on them to pick several cells that are not contiguous.

• To select all cells in the worksheet, click in the upper right corner to the left of "A."

How to Fill Cells with Data

To type data into a cell, click it and start typing. What you write appears in the Formula Bar as well. When entering dates, if the year component of the date is left blank, Excel defaults to the current year as the default.

You may modify the contents of a cell either from the Formula bar or directly from within the cell. If you choose a cell and click inside the Formula Bar, you may change it directly from the Formula Bar. When you're through typing, hit Enter or click inside another cell. Double-click inside a cell to modify it, or select the cell and use the F2 key to edit it immediately.

Each cell has its formatting. The format of a cell in Excel informs Excel how to display its information. The format of a cell may differ from the contents of the cell.

For example, suppose you typed 8.9521 into a cell. On the other hand, Excel will display 8.95 in that worksheet cell if the cell was set to only display two decimal places. However, when conducting computations that use that cell, Excel will continue to utilize the true cell value that you entered, 8.9521.

How to Propagate the Contents of Cells

Data can be propagated or filled from one cell to subsequent cells in a variety of ways. Let's start with two common keyboard keys for filling down and filling to the right:

• To fill neighboring cells with the cell contents above, select the data cell and the cells to be filled, then press Ctrl + D to fill down (the Ctrl key and the D key).

• Then select the cell holding the data and the cells that need to be filled and press Ctrl + R (the Ctrl and the R keys together) to fill nearby cells with what is now displayed in the selected cell to the left.

When you click on a cell containing data to be copied, hover your mouse over the cell's bottom right corner until the cursor changes to a thin plus sign (+) or a dark square, and then move the cursor up, down, left, or right, the cells will fill with data.

It will be increased by one when the Fill Handle is used to copy data containing dates, numbers, periods, or any other custom-made series instead of just copying the information. If you want to display the months of the year in column A, for example, enter January in cell A1, move the Fill Handle down to cell A12, and the months will appear in column A in chronological order!

How to Copy and Move the Contents of Cells

	Microsoft Excel - Book2				
	File Edit View Insert Format Tools Data V				

	A	B	C	D	
1					
2	Sales	34567			
3	Expenses	1234			
4		33,333			
5					

B4   *fx* =SUM(B2-B3)

marching ants appear during the copy process

To relocate the contents of a cell, right-click it and select Cut, then right-click in the new position and select Paste. Select Copy from the menu bar when you right-click a cell's contents. Then paste the contents into a new cell. You can copy a cell's contents as stated above, but you can also paste and fill many neighboring cells. To paste in a block of cells:

1. In one corner, click and hold the left mouse button.
2. Swipe the pointer across to the other corner while holding the mouse button down until just the cells you wish to fill are highlighted.
3. Right-click and select Paste from the menu.

Press the ESC key or start typing in a new cell to erase the old cell's animated border.

How to Add and Remove Rows and Columns in a Table

In a spreadsheet, right-click on a row number and select Insert to add a new row. Excel always inserts the row that was clicked on ABOVE the one that was clicked. Press the F4 key to insert each new row if you wish to keep inserting rows.

To delete a row, right-click on the row number and select Delete from the menu that appears. By marking adjacent rows before clicking Erase, you may delete them all at once. Non-contiguous rows can also be selected by holding the CTRL key down while clicking Delete. Do not use the Delete key on your keyboard if you want to erase the contents of a single cell and not an entire row of data. New column. The column that was clicked on is always inserted to the LEFT of the column that was clicked on in Excel. After entering the first column, use the F4 key to add more columns, just as you would with rows.

To remove a column, right-click on the letter of the column and select Delete. By marking adjacent columns before clicking Erase, you may delete them all at once. You can choose non-contiguous columns by pressing and holding the CTRL-key. Don't press the Delete key on your keyboard if you want to erase the contents of one cell and not the contents of the full column.

How to Protect a Spreadsheet by Locking Cells

There are two ways to avoid unintentionally overwriting or deleting critical cell content. The cell must first be locked. The worksheet must also be password-protected. You owe yourself to understand which cells to lock and which worksheet protection settings to use if you have any valuable data or complicated formulae you don't want to lose because data DOES get mistakenly wiped(!).

Microsoft Excel offers many built-in functions that may boost productivity and provide outcomes that math formulae alone can't always match.

Don't be alarmed if you see ##### in a cell. It's simply Excel's method of informing you that the column must be made wider for the cell contents to show. Placing the cursor on the right-hand side of the column header and dragging the right-hand column edge until the data appears.

3. TOP FEATURES OF MS EXCEL

A host of new big data technologies have evolved to analyze, alter, and display data in the last ten years. Despite this, Microsoft Excel remains the go-to software for knowledge workers trying to make sense of data after 30 years. Microsoft CEO Satya Nadella insists that Excel is still the best Microsoft software, and 750 million knowledge workers worldwide back him up.

We've been teaching and testing Microsoft Excel for a decade, and according to a poll of several hundred office workers, we spend more than 10% of our working life spreadsheeting, and for those in R&D or finance, it's closer to 30%, or 2.5 hours a day.

Consider what would happen if a significant percentage of the global workforce were a bit more adept at utilizing the app. It would save time and increase production.

If you're learning how to use Microsoft Excel for the first time, you'll undoubtedly have many questions regarding the program's features. Because, let's face it, Excel, despite its many benefits, can be a difficult program to master. When your most annoying reporting duties at work resemble nails, it's like a hammer.

Excel includes several strong functions that can help you save time while producing spreadsheets, in addition to outstanding Excel features like flash fill, pivot tables, and conditional formatting. Invest some time in studying Excel so you can create and manage complicated reports and do what-if analyses on data like a pro!

Here are some key Excel functions to master today to help you get started.

The SUM Function

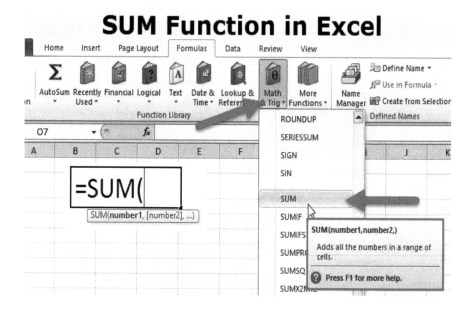

How to sum a row or column is probably one of the first Excel operations you'll master. Know that by selecting the last cell in a row or column and pressing Alt +, you may perform these tasks in seconds?

The sum function is the most often used in Excel when it comes to calculating data. This function sums a set of integers in a certain set of cells. This means you won't have to enter a long, complicated formula to determine the total of all the data you'll require. Because of its popularity,

Microsoft Excel has a button dedicated to this feature in subsequent versions.

To use this function, type the formula in the function bar and highlight the cells you wish to sum before pressing "Enter." You must also be cautious when highlighting cells, as Excel will add up whatever you enter. If this happens, click the "Undo" option to restore the settings to their previous state.

"=SUM" is the syntactic formula for the sum function (number1, number2, etc.).

The sum function for cells C2 through C7 in this picture is calculated using the formula "=SUM(C2:C7)," yielding 33161.

The TEXT Function

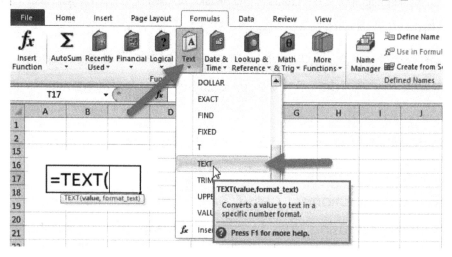

A text function is a handy tool for converting a date (or a number) to a text string in a certain format. It belongs to the string formulas group since it transforms numerical values into strings. When people need to see numeric data in an understandable style, it comes in useful. It's important to remember that the "TEXT" formula can only convert numeric numbers to text. As a result, it's impossible to compute the outcomes.

"=TEXT" (value, format text) is the syntactic formula for the text function.

• The term "value" refers to the specific number you want to convert to text.

• "Format text" specifies the conversion format.

The user uses a text formula to determine the abbreviated day for the date "=TEXT (B2, "ddd")" in this example.

The VLOOKUP Function

	A	B	C	D	E	F	G	H	I	J
			COUNTIF ▼ ⋮ ✕ ✓ *fx* =VLOOKUP(H2,B3:E9,4,FALSE)						
1										
2		ID	First Name	Last Name	Salary		ID	53		
3		72	Emily	Smith	$64,901		Salary	=VLOOKUP(H2,B3:E9,4,FALSE)		
4		66	James	Anderson	$70,855					
5		14	Mia	Clark	$188,657					
6		30	John	Lewis	$97,566					
7		53	Jessica	Walker	$58,339					
8		56	Mark	Reed	$125,180					
9		79	Richard	Lopez	$91,632					
10										

VLookup is a useful Excel feature that is sometimes ignored. It will come in handy when users need to locate certain data in a huge table. VLookup may also be used to search your sheet for people, phone numbers, or particular data. The VLookup function makes this procedure faster and more efficient than manually searching for names and scrolling through hundreds of records.

"=VLOOKUP" (lookup value, table array, col index num, *range lookup*) is the VLookup formula.
• The data you're looking for is called "lookup value."

• The data column where you wish to narrow your search is "table array."

• "col index num" is the table column number from which you wish to get a value.

• The "range lookup" option allows you to search for an exact match of your lookup value without having to sort the database.

The AVERAGE Function

IRR		▼	:	×	✓	*fx*	=AVERAGE(LARGE(B5:F5,{1,2,3}))

▲	A	B	C	D	E	F	G	H	I

AVERAGE Function

Test 1	Test 2	Test 3	Test 4	Test 5	Top 3 Averages
100	70	10	88	79	=AVERAGE(LARGE(B5:F5,{1,2,3}))
90	90	90	80	89	90.00
89	60	77	87	56	84.33
89	80	88	86	65	87.67
78	80	55	82	78	80.00

An average function is a fantastic tool for calculating the average value of a group of cells. It's similar to the sum function in that it's often used in spreadsheets to compute and analyze data. Averaging is used to get the "arithmetic mean" of a group of cells. Excel also contains the median and mode functions in addition to the average function.

The average function's syntactic formula is "AVERAGE" (number1, number2, etc.).

• The first number in the range where you want the average is referred to as "Number 1."

• The average range is often referred to as "Number 2." You can obtain a total of 255 cells as an average.

Additional examples include:

"=AVERAGE (A2:A10)" calculates the average of the values in cells A2 through A10.

"=AVERAGE (B2: B10, 7)" calculates the average of the numbers in cells B2 through B10, as well as the number 7.

The CONCATENATE Function

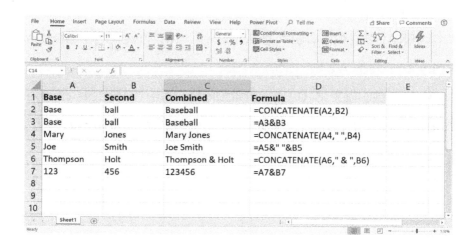

This function is useful for combining data from many cells. The concatenate function, unlike the merge tool, which physically merges two or more cells into a single cell, mixes the contents of the merged cells. The concatenate function has been replaced by the Concat function in the most recent version of Excel (2016), and it will be integrated with more future versions of Excel.

The concatenate function's syntax formula is "CONCATENATE" (text1, [text2...text n]), where "Text1, Text2...text n" are the data you wish to merge.

INDEX-MATCH

MATCH	▾	⊡	✕ ✓ ƒx	=INDEX(B2:D10,MATCH(G4,B2:B10,0),H6)			

◢	A	B	C	D	E	F	G	H	I
1	No.	First Name	Age	City					
2	1	Aaron	12	London		Search :			
3	2	Fabia	65	Sion					
4	3	Barney	31	Chicago		First Name :	Freddy		
5	4	Dario	7	Paris					
6	5	Alan	18	Zurich		Age (2), City (3) :	3		
7	6	Freddy	23	Monaco					
8	7	Ashley	46	San Francisco		Result :			
9	8	Bob	49	New York					
10	9	Alex	57	Geneva		=INDEX(B2:D10,MATCH(G4,B2:B10,0),H6)			
11									

INDEX and MATCH are the most commonly used and powerful lookup techniques in Excel, aside from VLOOKUP (which searches up a value in one column and returns a similar value from another column). These functions are useful on their own, but their entire power is revealed when you combine them. Combining INDEX and MATCH allows you to retrieve the data you need from a big collection quickly and precisely. Not only will mastering these functions make you appear like an Excel expert to your coworkers and boss, but it will also make a boring, routine activity quick and easy. The following is how these functions work:

VLOOKUP is a fantastic feature; however, it has certain drawbacks. It can only search up values in the left-to-right direction. In the lookup table, the lookup value must be on the left. INDEX and MATCH allow you to search up a value independent of its location in the lookup table.

Assume you have a spreadsheet with a product list. There are columns for "Product Number," "Profit," "Product Name," and "Revenue." You have a list of product names on another spreadsheet, and you want to see how much profit each product has produced. In this case, we're looking for the profit using the product name (our search value). VLOOKUP would not function since the product name is to the right of the profit. INDEX and MATCH are ideal in this situation.

The syntax would be as follows:

=INDEX(Profit column,MATCH(Lookup Value,Product Name column,0)) =INDEX(Profit column,MATCH(Lookup Value,Product Name column,0)) =INDEX(Profit

Here's a simple way to recall how it works:

=INDEX (Column from which I want a return value, MATCH (My Lookup Value, Column from which I want to Lookup, Enter "0")) (An exact match is zero; you may also match against less than (-1) or larger than (1).)

INDEX and MATCH appear complicated at first view and even at second glance. It takes some getting accustomed to, but it is more versatile and powerful than a VLOOKUP—one of Excel's most vital functions, without a doubt.

It's Simple To Stay Focused At Work And Get Things Done Quickly
Don't miss this guide with special ideas to sharpen your concentration and help you work more effectively if you want to increase your productivity.

Remove Duplicates

This is easy to use. Remove Duplicates does exactly what it says on the tin: it eliminates duplicates from any set of data. Remove the values you wish to dedupe and arrange them on another sheet, according to our advice. It's in the Data Tools area of the Ribbon, on the Data tab. Conditional Formatting is the way to go to highlight duplication. Alt HL is the shortcut to get you there. (You may also locate it under Styles on the Home ribbon.)

Freeze Panes

Have you ever scrolled through a long table of data and lost track of which columns are which? The solution is to use Freeze Panes. You can choose to freeze simply the first row, the first column, or any combination of the two. Determine the columns and rows of the region to be frozen. Then choose the cell to the right of those columns and freeze Panes in the View tab's Window section underneath those rows. Alt WF is the keyboard shortcut.

4. BASIC FORMULAS AND FUNCTIONS

For beginners to become extremely skilled in financial analysis, they must first master the basic Excel formulae. Microsoft Excel is widely regarded as the industry standard in data analysis software. Microsoft's spreadsheet tool is one of the most popular among investment bankers and financial analysts in terms of data processing, financial modeling, and presentation. This section will provide you a rundown of basic Excel functions as well as a list of them.

1. Include a header and a footer
We may retain the header and footer in our spreadsheet document using MS Excel.

2. Replace and Find Command
MS Excel enables us to locate required data (text and numbers) within a worksheet and replace old data with new data.

3. Password Security

Allows users to encrypt their workbooks with a password to protect them from unauthorized access.

4. Filtering of Data

Filtering is a quick and simple method of locating and manipulating a subset of data in a range. Only the rows that satisfy the criteria you set for a column appear in a filtered range. For filtering ranges in MS Excel, there are two commands:

• AutoFilter; this provides a selection-based filter for simple criteria.

• Advanced Filter; for criteria that are more difficult to define.

5. Data Sorting

The process of organizing data in a logical order is known as data sorting. We may sort data in ascending or descending order in MS Excel.

6. Built-in formulae

MS Excel has got many built-in formulae for sum, average, minimum, etc.

We can utilize such formulas according to our needs.

7. Create different charts (Pivot Table Report)

MS Excel allows us to make various charts, including bar graphs, pie charts, line graphs, and more. This allows us to evaluate and compare data quickly.

8. Edits the result automatically

If any modifications are made in any of the cells, MS Excel immediately updates the result.

9. Formula Auditing

We may use blue arrows to graphically illustrate or trace the links between cells and formulae with formula auditing. We can follow the antecedents (cells that supply data to a certain cell) or the dependents (cells that are reliant on a specific cell) (the cells that depend on the value in a specific cell).

There are five popular ways to enter basic Excel formulae while evaluating data. Each method has its own set of benefits. As a result, before we get into the major formulae, let's go through those techniques so you can set up your preferred workflow right away.

Inserting a formula into a cell is a simple process

Inserting basic Excel formulae is as simple as typing a formula in a cell or using the formula bar. Typically, the procedure begins with an equal sign followed by the name of an Excel function.

Excel is clever in that it displays a pop-up function suggestion as you start typing the function name. You'll choose your preference from this list. Do not, however, hit the Enter key. Instead, hit the Tab key to continue inserting other selections. Otherwise, you could get an incorrect name error, which looks like '#NAME?'. Pick the cell again and complete your function in the formula bar.

Using the Formulas Tab's Insert Function Option

The Excel Insert Function dialogue box is all you need to complete control over your function insertion. Select Insert Function from the first drop-down option on the Formulas tab. The dialogue box will include all of the elements you'll need to do your financial analysis.

Formula Tab: Selecting a Formula from One of the Groups This choice is for individuals who want to get to their favorite features rapidly. To find this option, go to the Formulas tab and choose your chosen group. To open a sub-menu with a list of functions, click. You can then choose your preferred option. If your desired group isn't shown on the tab, click the More Functions option - it's most likely buried there.

Using AutoSum Option

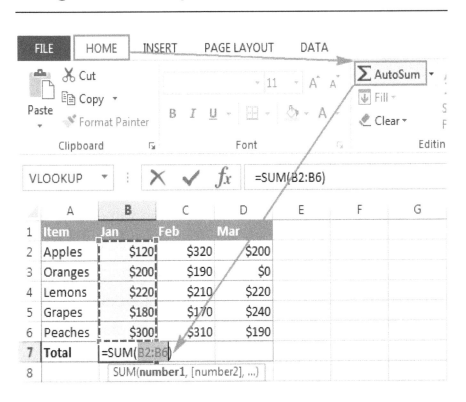

The AutoSum function is your go-to solution for short and everyday jobs. So, go to the Home page and choose the AutoSum option in the far-right corner. Then click the caret to reveal more formulae that were previously concealed. This option is also accessible after the Insert Function option in the Formulas tab.

Use Recently Used Tabs for a Quick Insert

Use the Recently Used option instead of retyping your most recent formula if you find it tedious. It's on the Formulas tab, right next to AutoSum, as the third menu choice.

You've made the decision. You switched from Evernote to Notion after hearing about the buzzy productivity software. You're looking forward to this new chapter in note-taking. You've learned Notion's fundamentals, built a GTD to-do list, and even a Personal Wiki. As you sit down to create your first If Statement, you expect to see a familiar Excel-like structure, but then it occurs to you: Where are the cells? Why aren't these property types all the same? And why do these formulas appear to be so dissimilar?

5. Advanced Formulas, Features, And Functions

Today's business requires the use of a variety of software and tools to manage and operate effectively. In business jargon, the technologies are utilized to save time and money by providing rapid analytical findings. There are several tools available for a range of companies, the most prominent and well-known of which is Microsoft Office Excel, a tool that every business needs.

Excel's outstanding collection of abilities to execute functions and complex excel formulas is not a myth; it is a declared truth that Excel assists small, medium, and big size organizations in storing, maintaining, and analyzing data into useful information. The program handles and covers different aspects of a business on its own, such as accounting, budgeting, and sales, among others.

Excel is one of the most significant and helpful pieces of software, and its prominent features allow you to perform the following.

Prepare magnificent charts

An excel sheet, as we all know, has a large number of grids. These sheets are restricted to numbers or data input, but they may be used to visualize prospective data using advanced Excel formulas and functions. The data is sorted, filtered, and structured using the functions assigned to the rows and columns. As a visual display for greater understanding, the information from the assigning and arranging is transformed into charts.

The set of statistics is difficult to comprehend and draw a conclusion from. The pie charts, grouped columns, and graphs make analyzing and interpreting data in a short amount of time a lot simpler. Excel is a powerful tool for producing company reports and marketing materials. Conditional formatting is made easier with visual aids. Colors, tints, italics, bold, and other formatting choices assist distinguish rows and columns so you can find data quickly and save time. Because of the color difference, a user can quickly identify the appropriate column and row in a large data set. The formatting tab makes it simple to enter a color scheme.

Identifying trends

When it comes to developing a plan by observing patterns and forecasting the next, the statistical effect in a firm is enormous. Average lines can be given to charts, graphs, clustered columns, and other visual representations. The average line aids an analyst in determining the main trend in the data set. It can quickly comprehend the format's main points.

The projection may be used to take the trend or average lines a step farther. Future trends can be predicted using these projections in the visual depiction. The prediction can aid in the creation of new initiatives that will propel the company to new heights of success.

Bring anything

The software's versatility may handle almost any form of data. Spreadsheets, documents, and even pictures can be used. Access is made easier when all of the data is placed under one roof for convenience. In Excel, importing any data is a breeze. The Insert Tab assists the user in data aggregation.

Excel's cloud function has elevated its use to new heights. Office 365 Business and its premium edition may be accessed from various devices, making it easier to do business. This software allows for remote working by coordinating papers and sheets.

Advanced excel formula and functions

Excel offers a plethora of useful uses. The simple form is used by 95% of the users. For sophisticated computations, there are functions and advanced excel formulas that may be employed. The functions are meant to make it simple to search up and prepare a vast amount of data, whereas the advanced excel formula is used to extract new information from a specific data collection.

Excel's OFFSET Formula

This sophisticated excel function, when used with other functions like SUM or AVERAGE, may give computations a dynamic feel. It's excellent for putting continuous rows into a database that already exists. OFFSET Excel gives us a range to fill in with the reference cell, the number of rows, and the number of columns. Ex. If we have a list of workers' salaries sorted by employee ID and want to calculate the average of the top five employees in the company, we may use the formula below. The formula below returns salaried every time.

Excel formulas for LEFT, MID, and RIGHT

This sophisticated excel formula may be used to extract a specified substring from a text. It could be appropriate for our needs. Ex. We may apply the LEFT formula in Excel with the column name and second parameter as 5 to extract the first five characters from Employee Name.

Excel's CONCATENATE Formula

One of the equations that may be utilized with numerous versions is this excel advanced function. This sophisticated Excel formula allows us to combine many text strings into a single one. For example, suppose we wish to display both the employee ID and the employee name in a single column.

SUMIF Formula in Excel

When using the sum or count function in some studies, you may need to filter some observations. This sophisticated excel SUMIF function in excel comes to our rescue in such situations. After filtering them based on the conditions specified in this sophisticated excel formula, it adds up all of the observations. What if we want to know the total salary of workers with employee IDs higher than 3?

IF AND Formula in Excel

There are numerous situations where flags must be created depending on limitations. The basic syntax of IF is familiar to all of us. This advanced excel IF function makes a new field based on a constraint on an existing field. But what if we need to take into account many columns while constructing a flag? Ex. In the example below, we want to identify all workers with a salary of more than $50,000 but an employee ID of more than three.

Excel MATCH Formula

When there is a certain text or number in the provided range, this Excel advanced formula provides the row or column number. In the example below, we're looking for "Rajesh Ved" in the Employee Name field.

Excel VLOOKUP Formula

One of the most often used formulae in Excel is the advanced excel function. It is mostly due to the formula's simplicity and its use in seeking a certain value from other tables that share a similar variable. Assume you have two tables with pay and name information for a company's employees, with Employee ID as the main column. In Table A, you wish to extract the salary from Table B.

VLOOKUP is divided into three categories:

1. You cannot have the main column to the right of the column for which you want the value from another table to be populated. Employee Salary cannot be placed before Employee ID in this scenario.

2. The first value in the duplicated values in Table B's main column will be filled in the cell.

3. If you add a new column to the database (for example, before Employee Salary in Table B), the formula's output may change depending on the position you specified in the formula.

#2 - Excel INDEX Formula

This sophisticated Excel formula is used to determine the value of a cell in a table depending on the number of rows, columns, or both in the table.

6. PIVOT TABLES

When it comes to displaying bespoke charts or tables with a lot of data, pivot tables may save you a lot of time. In reality, Microsoft has made the process of creating them quite simple and uncomplicated. Still, certain methods can be used once a table has been created to assist the financial modeler in creating an array of summary tables. Said, pivot tables allow you to quickly and easily show a wide range of data in a summary table style.

To get started, a financial modeler would select PivotTable and PivotChart Report from the Data menu or PivotTable Wizard from the PivotTable toolbar's PivotTable menu. In any instance, Microsoft lets you choose where the data for the pivot table analysis should be stored. To make things easy, you're probably going to utilize the default configuration (Microsoft Office Excel list or database). The second step is to identify the cells that should be included in the study. You may either use your mouse or keyboard to capture the database, or you can specify the range and write in its name. Finally, you may insert the table into an existing sheet or create a new one. That's all there is to a basic pivot table.

Setting this up has no actual mystery or difficulty since, as previously said, Microsoft did a wonderful job of making it simple.

Consider the following scenario: two data points must be captured. You might wish to discover which firms sold the most widgets in a simple pivot table. The firms are listed in the left-hand column, while the number of units sold is shown in the right-hand column. But what if you wanted to know not just how many widgets were sold but also how much they cost?

Right-click and then click on the wizard again in your current pivot table. You'll notice a box labeled "Layout," which you'll select. This is where you may drag several elements into the pivot table's "data" box, such as the number of units sold and total sales. You will now see a pivot table with two pieces of information for each firm after hitting the "Finish" button. You may also drag data into the column area to split data by firm name and, possibly, the day of the week on which the sales were made. This is as simple as dragging and dropping - it doesn't get any simpler than that.

If you enjoy formulae and want to construct a customer table, you can use =GETPIVOTDATA(data field, pivot table, [field1], [item1], [field2], [item2],...) in conjunction with a pivot table. It is a simple formula that can be used in conjunction with a pivot table for those who enjoy formulae and want to construct a customer table.

In this scenario, up to 14 field/item references can be used in the same document. Naturally, the pivot table refers to the pivot table you are currently using. The data field refers to the total or count of anything, such as the number of widgets in your pivot table. The field/item combinations relate to the label of the information you're looking for, followed by the search item itself. If you had a pivot table with color-coded vehicle sales, and your data column was "sum of sales price," you'd get the total of all black automobiles sold in your database.

This is intended to provide a basic overview of pivot tables. I learned more about how to use the various capabilities by experimenting with different formats and data combinations. You will have a basic knowledge if you spend a few hours breaking down a pivot table, understanding the layout button, and working with the GETPIVOTDATA formula. Once you've done so, you'll be able to see how a large amount of data in a spreadsheet may be split down and presented in simple but powerful summary tables.

What Is a Pivot Table and How Do I Make One?

Do you use Excel to work with data? Do you make use of pivot tables? It's possible that you aren't because you don't know-how. You could even be awestruck by them and believe your Excel abilities aren't up to the task of handling these enigmatic masterpieces. The opposite could not be further from the truth. I can't think of anything that has as much unjustified mystery around it as Pivot Tables. Let me demonstrate how to make one from scratch. Explaining the processes is far more difficult than incorporating them into your workbook.

The notion of pivot tables hasn't changed much since they were first introduced, but Microsoft has made modifications to how they're created with each new version of Excel. Because I'm writing about Office 2010, things could look a bit different on your screen. Begin by locating some facts that you want to summarize. It must be properly set up in a table or database.

1. Select any cell in your data by clicking on it.

2. In the Tables group on the Insert ribbon, click the top half of the Pivot Table button.

3. A dialog window will appear. A flashing line should be drawn around your data to highlight the cells that Excel believes you want to summarize. You can change this if necessary. For the last option, select New Sheet and click OK.

A Field List pane should be on the right side of your screen, with a box that states Pivot Table # and some text and images on the left. Many first-time authors acquire a scared expression in their eyes at this point, close the workbook without saving modifications, and deny they ever existed.

Imagine an attendance record like the ones used in school to obtain a rudimentary idea of the elements of a Pivot Table. The dates are usually placed in the first row (Column Labels), and the names of the pupils are placed in the first column along the rows (the Row Labels). To signify whether the student attended or not, a mark is put in the crossing cells (Values). Although this example does not exactly reflect how data is collected in Excel, it fits our goal of highlighting the regions inside a Pivot Table.

We may return to building one now that we know the areas:

4. Look to the right of your screen for the Field List. Your data's field headers should be in the box at the top. Any header you place in the Column Labels box will span the top of your table. Any heading you drag into the Row Labels box will appear on the table's left side. Any heading you drag into the Values box will be summed up in the middle cells. Totals will be displayed if the header you drag represents numbers, but the count function will be utilized for the value if the header represents a field of text.

5. Drag and drop headers from any of the boxes into the Choose Fields box if you wish to delete them.

6. The Row and Column labels can have several fields. If you slide these headers around to modify their order, you'll get a whole new appearance. Only insert headers in the Row Labels box to make a linear table; leave the Column Labels box empty.

Drag field heads in and out of different places to see what occurs is the easiest approach to get started with Pivot Tables. The sort of table you want to make is determined by the information you're looking for. It can be a trial-and-error procedure. Even though this part scratches the surface of what Pivot Tables can achieve, I highly encourage learning more about this valuable Excel feature. You never know what you could be capable of.

Helpful Tips

1. You'll see contextual ribbons (Pivot Table Tools) with two tabs as long as your Pivot Table is active (Options, Design). This is where you'll find all of the Pivot Table tools. These tools will vanish if you don't click on the Pivot Table or the Pivot Table box on the left of your screen when you initially insert a Pivot Table.

2. A good database may contain empty cells, but no rows or columns should be empty.

3. If the Pivot Table Field List on the right of your screen is unintentionally closed, click the Field List button in the Show group of the Options tab of the Pivot Table Tools to reopen it.

4. Your information is on a separate sheet in your workbook. To find it, look at the tabs at the bottom of the page.

5. For the same data, you may create several Pivot Tables.

6. If you make any changes to the data and want them to appear in your Pivot Table, you must manually update/refresh it. This offers you the option of leaving the table alone while you input more raw data.

a. From the right-click menu, select Refresh (right-click on the Pivot Table).

b. Select Refresh from the Data group on the Pivot Table Tools' Options ribbon.

A pivot table is a table that is used to hold a simplified version of a data set's summary. Rows, columns, data fields, and pages make up the table. These movable components allow the user to expand, isolate, sum, and group-specific data in real-time. This table allows the viewer to see the differences in a large amount of data. Microsoft Excel, it's quite useful for organizing enormous amounts of data.

Working of the Table

Each column's heading in a pivot table becomes an editable data option. Data-containing columns may be easily deleted, added to, or changed about the table. Long spreadsheets of raw data may be turned into user-friendly and useful summaries here. The information may be summarized in several ways, including using frequencies and averages. The advantages of using a pivot table in Excel are listed below.

Simple to Use

The fact that pivot tables are simple to use is a significant benefit. By moving columns to different areas of the table, you may quickly summarize data. With a click of the mouse, you may rearrange the columns in any way you like.

Data Analysis Made Simple

Excel pivot tables allow you to manage huge amounts of data in a single operation. These tables allow you to deal with a vast quantity of data while only seeing a few data columns. This makes vast amounts of data easier to analyze.

Easy Summary of Data

Another significant advantage of pivot tables is that they simplify summarizing data out of thousands of rows and columns of unstructured data—the table aids in creating a clear summary. These tables may condense a lot of information into a little area. The information can be summarized in an easy-to-understand style. Users may name and organize the data in whatever manner they choose, and they can rearrange the rows and columns to suit their needs.

Find Data Patterns

You may use Excel pivot tables to generate customized tables from big data sets. Manipulation of data in this way will aid in the discovery of recurrent patterns in the data if any exist. This, in turn, will aid in the precise forecasting of data.

Quick Report Creation

One of the most useful characteristics of excel pivot tables is that they make it easier to produce reports. This removes the need to manually produce reports for long periods. Aside from that, the table allows you to include connections to external sources in the report you've produced.

Assists in making quick decisions Making

A pivot table is a useful Excel reporting tool because it allows users to quickly examine data and make choices based on it. This is a major benefit in the industrial sector, where making precise and rapid judgments is critical.

Advantages and Disadvantages of Pivot Tables

Users can summarize or restructure rows or columns of data using pivot tables, which are software tools. They're most commonly seen in database tables and spreadsheets, and they let you get information from a report without having to change the file.

Here are some of the benefits and drawbacks of utilizing a pivot table in your spreadsheets.

List of Advantages for Pivot Tables

1. They allow you to see how the data works.

Pivot tables are one of the few tools that can give users deep insights into analytics data. This application may produce many reports from the same gathered data in a single file.

2. It is compatible with SQL exports.

Using Microsoft Excel to create the pivot table, the tool can function with any SQL export.

3. Data can be segmented more easily.

The use of pivot tables makes it easy to segregate data collected in a spreadsheet or database.

4. You may generate data right away.

Instant data may be produced using this tool, whether you write equations directly into the pivot table or rely on formulae.

Pivot Tables Have a Long List of Drawbacks

1. It is a time-consuming endeavor.

In most cases, pivot tables can provide the data needed to analyze metrics, but in many cases, the tool lacks computation alternatives. That implies the data must be manually computed or equations manually entered, both of which take time.

2. No automatic updates are available.

Unless users run their reports every day utilizing their pivot tables, they are flying blind regarding metrics and analytics. Programs utilizing pivot tables do not provide a readily summarized display of data.

3. Data presentation on older machines might be difficult.

Older technology may struggle to create the needed data if the spreadsheet or database is particularly large. Some users' equipment may even fail due to the demands being too great for its processing capability.

4. Learning them takes time.

It's easy to learn how to use a pivot table, but you'll need to find out how to make the data meaningful. When it comes to pivot tables, most spreadsheets don't focus on delivering a pleasant user experience.

For tiny datasets, pivot tables are advantageous, but for big spreadsheets, they are disadvantageous. Taking these advantages and downsides into consideration, it becomes much easier to organize and utilize spreadsheet-based data.

7. CHARTS AND GRAPHS WITH MS EXCEL

Microsoft Excel is a popular spreadsheet application used by a wide range of businesses across the world. Its strength comes in its capacity to process massive amounts of data, making it ideal for various industries such as banking, business, finance, statistics, and sales and places where big amounts of data must be analyzed.

When visualizing numerical data, the adage "a picture is worth a thousand words" is quite accurate. Humans sometimes struggle to comprehend numbers provided in a table, but most of us find it far simpler to comprehend numerical data presented in the form of a chart or graph. With its vast selection of charts, Microsoft Excel takes full use of this — and the good news is that they're easy to make!

Excel comes with several graph kinds, each of which is tailored to a certain function. A column or line chart is ideal for seeing values moving over time; a pie chart is probably better for seeing the distribution within a population, such as market share or sales by department.

Stock, bubble, scatter, and radar charts are among the chart styles dedicated to statistical analysis; however, they are more specialized and are not included here.

How to create an Excel Graph

- Open the spreadsheet with the data you wish to graph.
- Make sure you are on the worksheet that contains the data
- Highlight the data that will be used to create the chart by dragging over it with your mouse
- Tip: it is better not to include totals for the data as it will skew the results
- Include the labels for both the columns and rows and the data in between.
- In pre-2007 versions, go to the Insert menu and choose Chart
- In post-2007 versions, go to the Insert tab and click on the appropriate chart type from the Chart group
- Or in any version, use the keyboard shortcut - press the F11 key!

Excel will create a new graph based on the date you selected. Using the keyboard shortcut would place the graph on its page named "Chart1".

It is easy to move or edit the chart by first selecting it, choosing Chart Type or Chart Options, and working through the wizard.

Drawing a graph in Excel is a fairly easy thing to do these days. First, let me clarify that charts and graphs in Excel are the same things. There is no actual drawing to do it is a matter of a few simple clicks, which makes Microsoft Office so uncomplicated to use. I include a little exercise for you to follow to create a line graph to see how it works. For this exercise, you can build a fictitious Spreadsheet and input bogus data, or you can utilize an existing file if you have one.

Take these easy steps to get started.
• Don't leave any blank rows or columns between data entries. When creating your spreadsheet, start by describing the data in one column and then entering the data in the column to the right. If there are many data sets, Give each data sequence a title, then fill the

columns with unique information. Then you'll need to choose the Graph Data.

• Drag and highlight the cells containing the data you want to graph with your mouse.

1. In Microsoft Excel 2007, on the ribbon Insert by clicking the button.

2. Select a graph type from the Chart category by clicking on it.

Selecting the Most Appropriate Chart Type for Your Data: In general, pie charts are only utilized when the number of categories is limited enough that the relative sizes of the various slices can be identified. Use a column chart for several categories. Use a line chart for data that must be presented in a specific sequence. Keep in mind that a line chart will change data that happens at irregular periods. X-Y Scatter Charts are useful for plotting two numeric values against each other and capturing data with irregular time intervals.

You may construct a custom chart based on the built-in chart types if you can't seem to locate one that matches your needs—combining two or more kinds in a single graph result in a combination chart.

The following are some factors to bear in mind when constructing your graph:

• There should be no more than three or four data series in a line graph.

• Gridlines should only be used to indicate approximate values, and they should be used rarely.

• When formatting, choose colors that will stand out on the printed edition.

• Keep text styles simple, so data doesn't get mixed up.

You now know how simple it is to create a graph and the many types of graphs and how to pick the proper type in Excel for better design. You may experiment with different fonts and colors to customize the look of your graph.

1. Enter your information into Excel.

To begin, enter your data into Excel. You might have exported the data from another source, such as marketing software or a survey service. Or perhaps you're typing it in by hand.

In the following example, Column A has a list of replies to the question, "Did inbound marketing demonstrate ROI?" and Columns B, C, and D include responses to the question, "Does your firm have a formal sales-marketing agreement?" FOR EXAMPLE, Column C, Row 2 shows that 49 percent of those with an SLA (service level agreement) believe inbound marketing has shown ROI.

2. Select one of the graph or chart options.

Charts and graphs in Excel include column (or bar) graphs, line graphs, pie graphs, scatter plots, and more. Examine how Excel recognizes each of them on the top navigation bar, as seen below:

Select Insert to see the chart and graph choices.

3. Highlight your data and enter the graph you want into the spreadsheet.

The data will be represented graphically in this example through the use of a bar graph. The following are the stages to creating a bar graph:

Draw a line through the data and insert the X and Y axis headers.

Navigate to the Insert tab and then to the Charts section, where you will see the column icon.

Select the graph you want from the dropdown menu that displays.

In this case, I chose the first two-dimensional column choice because I like the flat bar visual over the three-dimensional appearance. The resultant bar graph is shown below.

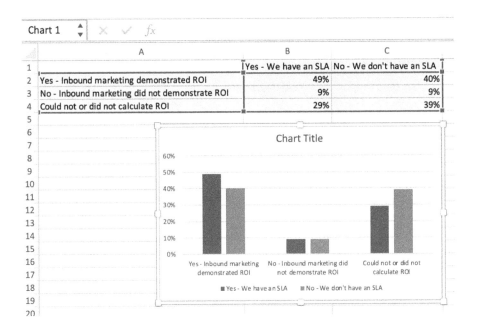

4. If required, switch the data on each axis to the other.

If you wish to change the data that shows on the X and Y axes, right-click on the bar graph, select Data, and then Switch Row/Column from the context menu. This will change how the axes convey which bits of information are in the list below. After finishing, click OK at the bottom of the page.

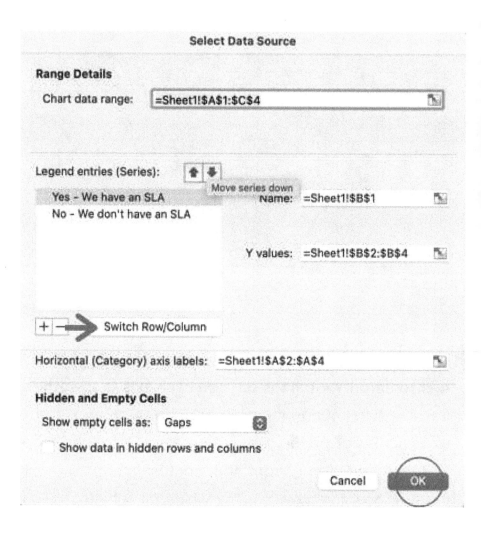

5. Change the style and colors of your data.

Click on the bar graph, then the Chart Design tab, to modify the arrangement of the labels and legend. You may select the arrangement for the chart title, axis titles, and legend here. In my example, I selected the option to display softer bar colors and legends underneath the chart.

Click on the legend to see the Format Legend Entry sidebar, as shown below. You may alter the fill color of the legend here, which will change the color of the columns. To format additional elements of your chart, click on them one at a time to bring up the relevant Format box.

6. Increase or decrease the size of your chart's legend and axis labels.

Depending on the style of graph or chart you pick, the size of your axis and legend labels may be a little small when you first create a graph in Excel (bar, pie, line, etc.) After you've finished your chart, you'll want to improve the legibility of the labels.

To enlarge the labels on your graph, click on them individually and, instead of exposing a new Format window, return to the Home tab in Excel's top navigation bar. Then, using the font style and size dropdown boxes, you may expand or decrease your chart's legend and axis labels to your satisfaction.

7. If desired, modify the Y-axis measurement settings.

To alter the type of measurement presented on the Y axis, open the Format Axis box by clicking on the Y-axis percentages in your chart. You may choose whether to display units from the Axis Options page or show percentages to 2 decimal places or 0 decimal places on the Y-axis.

Because my graph automatically sets the maximum percentage on the Y axis to 60%, I may want to alter it to 100% to display my data on a universal scale. To do so, I may alter the number from 0.6 to 1 by selecting the Maximum option — two fields down under Bounds in the Format Axis box.

The resulting graph would be modified to appear like this (I raised the font size of the Y-axis through the Home tab to show the difference):

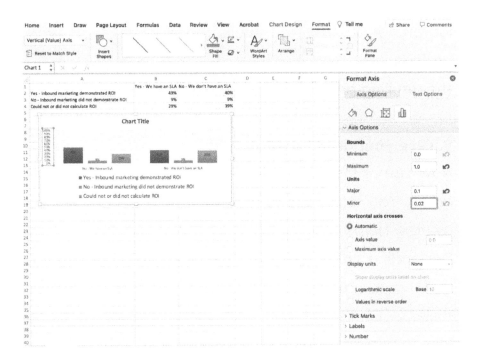

8. If necessary, reorder your data.

To arrange the data so that the respondents' responses show in reverse order, right-click on your graph and select Data to open the same choices box as in Step 3 above. This time, use the up and down arrows to reverse the order of your data on the chart, as shown below.

Changing more than two data lines can be done in ascending or descending order. To do so, select all of your data in the cells above your chart, click Data, and then Sort, as shown below. You can order by smallest to largest or largest to smallest, depending on your preferences.

The resulting graph would be as follows:

9. Give your graph a title.

Now comes the enjoyable and simple part: naming your graph. You may have found out how to accomplish this by now. Here's a straightforward clarifier.

Depending on the version of Excel you're using, the title that shows immediately after creating your chart will most likely be "Chart Title" or something similar. Click on "Chart Title" to display a typing cursor and then modify the label. The title of your chart may then be freely customized.

When you've found a title you like, click Home in the top navigation bar and utilize the font formatting choices to emphasize it. See the following choices, as well as my final graph:

10. Save your graph or chart as an image.

When your chart or graph is precise as you want it, save it as a picture instead of screenshotting it in the spreadsheet. This approach will provide you with a clean image of your chart that you can place into a PowerPoint presentation, Canva page, or any other visual design.

To save your excel graph as a photograph, right-click on it and choose Save as Picture...

Give your graph's snapshot a name in the dialogue box, choose where you want it saved on your computer, and select the file format. In this case, I'm exporting it to my desktop folder as a JPEG. Finally, click the Save button.

You will get a clear image of your graph or chart that you can include in any visual design.

Data Visualization Like a Pro

That was a breeze. You'll be able to rapidly construct charts and graphs that depict even the most complex data with this step-by-step guide. Try the same tutorial with various graph styles, such as a pie chart or line graph, to discover which format best conveys your data narrative.

8. TIPS AND SUGGESTIONS TO IMPROVE YOUR SKILLS

An Excel tutorial can help you acquire new abilities or enhance old ones. Excel is an application that you should be familiar with because there is so much you can accomplish with it. You'll be able to create spreadsheets in no time after you grasp how to set up the rows and columns. It's a much simpler procedure than most people assume when they first start using Excel.

What should I expect to get out of a basic Excel tutorial?

You should be able to understand formulae with a simple Excel formula in addition to learning how to build up rows and columns. In this manner, you may create some simple spreadsheets to fulfill your goals.

Using an Excel lesson to learn can assist in guarantee that the outcomes are professional. An Excel lesson will ensure that you understand the program's foundations and can generate professional-looking results.

You want to locate one that provides you with all of the facts in a straightforward manner. Sometimes you'll read a tutorial like this and have no idea what it's saying. Look for one that will guide you through every stage. Open your Excel software in a separate window so you may work on a spreadsheet simultaneously. This technique will assist you in remembering more of the information presented in the course.

How long will it take you to master the fundamentals of Excel?

If you utilize an Excel lesson, learning the basics of Excel won't take long. It will only take a few hours of your time. Even if you don't have much expertise with computers, you'll be able to produce some stunning spreadsheets. After you've completed the lesson, you'll want to put what you've learned into practice. Make sure you refer back to it as much as necessary. You'll be able to complete the spreadsheets you need without it before you realize it.

Excel Keyboard Shortcuts

The keyboard shortcuts in this piece will certainly come in helpful if you've ever been annoyed by having to stop what you're doing in Excel to grab the mouse to perform a common action. Microsoft Excel has many ways to conduct commands via the interface, but my personal preference is the keyboard shortcut for many of them. After reading these suggestions, you'll be racing through your spreadsheets and doing frequently repeated chores quickly and confidently!

Shortcut #1 - F6

When you don't know the normal keyboard shortcut for a task but don't want to stop and pick up your mouse, F6 is a nice little shortcut in Excel. F6 toggles between your active worksheet, the ribbon at the top of the screen, and the task pane at the bottom of the screen (including the zoom controls.) You can cycle to the portion of the screen you wish to work with by pressing F6 one or more times, then making choices with the arrow keys and Enter key.

Shortcut #2 - Ctrl+Z

Ctrl+Z will reverse whatever action you've just taken. Did you accidentally press the paste button when you wanted to paste formulae or values? No issue, using Ctrl+Z will take you back a step, allowing you to swiftly complete the task at hand.

Shortcut #3 - Ctrl+C

Although most people are familiar with this command, it is worth reiterating because it is so helpful when used with other keyboard commands. Ctrl+C copies the current cell or a specified range of cells so that you may paste them elsewhere in the Workbook.

Shortcut #4 - Alt+E, S

This is one of my personal favorites, yet just a few people are aware of it. The "Paste-Special" dialogue box may be accessed by pressing Alt+E and then S. From there, you have a few options: press V to pick Paste-Special-Values, T to select Paste-Special-Format, F to select Formulas, and so on. When you're in a rush, this is far more convenient than right-clicking with the mouse.

Shortcut #5 - Ctrl+Arrow Keys

This is the mark of a real Excel aficionado. You may get to the farthest end of a range of cells by holding down the Ctrl key and pressing one of the keyboard arrows. This is useful for rapidly accessing the bottom row of a huge dataset or switching from the far right to the far left of a worksheet.

Shortcut #6 - Shift+Ctrl+Arrow Keys

Adding shift to the mix, like shortcut #5, selects all cells from the one you're starting on to the target cell.

Shortcut #7 - Ctrl+PageUp/Dwn

This is a wonderful method to move through your workbook's different worksheets. This one gets a lot of usage from me.

As you can see, Excel has a plethora of simple keyboard shortcuts that can help you be more productive at work. This is only a sample of what's possible, but I hope it's been useful.

Import Data From A Website

A corporation or business has no choice but to go online in today's competitive marketplaces if they want to succeed. Businesses may reach a larger audience and give information that is difficult to incorporate in print advertisements or brochures by going online. They must first pick a website host before taking advantage of everything that online marketing has to offer. Choosing a host isn't as simple as some may believe. Before selecting, there are numerous variables to consider and certain characteristics that separate an adequate host from an exceptional one.

The spectrum of website hosts includes anything from free accounts to high-end hosting servers. Whatever choice you choose, keep in mind your business demands and your company's possibilities for expansion and growth, as these will help you select the best host for your needs.

Round the clock support

Maintaining touch with clients and associates, as well as minimizing sales losses, need 24-hour assistance. If an issue arises, you may report it, and it will be resolved quickly. If you don't have access to 24-hour assistance, your issues may be placed on a waiting list, and you may have to wait days for them to be resolved.

Bandwidth

The bigger the volume of data that can be transferred and the sooner your website opens, the higher your bandwidth. According to research, users quit a website that takes more than 10 seconds to load. To avoid needless problems, make sure your bandwidth surpasses your demands, especially if your company regularly employs video, music, or graphics.

Excessive storage space

Deciding on how much storage space you're going to need is much like choosing the size of your bandwidth. Your bandwidth requirements will be less than those of a huge website if your demands are simple, and you won't be employing video, audio, or massive graphics. To allow your firm to develop, it's a good idea to buy somewhat more space than you need or to make sure that your service has upgrading facilities.

Email

A hosting service that provides an email service is a better option than one without email facilities. Companies should have email addresses that are linked to their trading identities. This boosts their accessibility and trustworthiness in the eyes of their customers.

Additional domains

Even if your present needs only necessitate one domain name, having the ability to register additional domain names in the case of growth and expansion is critical.

Domain parking

A domain name parking service allows you to keep your domain name active by storing it on the host's server. When a company does not have its name servers, this functionality is used.

Site management tools

You must be able to confidently and easily administer your site whenever the need arises. You'll be able to change or update information on your site if you have the proper administration tools.

Guaranteed uptime of at least 99 percent is another crucial characteristic to look for in a website hosting server. Unreliable hosting might cost you money in terms of visitors and sales. Many providers provide free hosting because you allow advertisements to be placed on it in terms of free hosting. Pop-up ads are extremely harmful to your site because most consumers dislike them and avoid visiting sites with them. You may be limited in the size of icons and visuals you may use on free servers. They can also provide you a regulatory template that limits the design and content space you have.

There are no regulations that bind you to a certain website hosting provider indefinitely once you've made your decision. You are allowed to switch to a server you believe will be better suited for your organization if you find their service unsatisfactory or have network availability issues. On the other hand, changing servers is not a straightforward procedure and can be fraught with unanticipated difficulties. It's preferable to be more cautious while making your initial choice. As much as feasible, research a range of hosts. Consider what you might require in the future and make an informed selection that will benefit your company.

Spreadsheets aren't the only place to find a lot of helpful information. Such information is frequently found on websites, which are occasionally built database-friendly (like tables of information). If you've found any data online that you think might be useful to you or your organization, it's time to learn how to import it into Excel.

Why would you want to do something like this? It will allow you to play with the data "offline," without running up your bandwidth or download fees, if you're still paying for internet access by bandwidth consumption (not so popular for home, landline-based internet packages anymore, but quite common if you're accessing the web from a mobile device). You can also edit the data more readily than you can when it's on a webpage. Furthermore, you may import several data sets from other websites, allowing you to create your super spreadsheet. Assume you're a shipping firm (or even an individual eBay seller) that is aware that your preferred postal providers charge various fees for different nations. You believe it would be a good idea to download each site's table of services/prices so you can readily compare rates by the nation when you know you'll be shipping anything there. Very helpful. Here's how you'd go about doing that.

Excel is mostly made up of tables and cells. It's time to start importing if your desired website includes a table. You may instruct Excel to import all or just one table from a website. To achieve this, use the "id" property to give the names or numbers of the tables. Give each table its name or number (id).

Then, in Excel, choose the cell where you want the table data to begin, and then "obtain external data," followed by "new web query." Then type in the web address for the data, followed by the names of the tables (along with their ids) that you wish to import.

All of the data from the web has now been imported into your worksheet, where you may augment it using pivot tables, analyze it, and add functions to help you navigate it more simply. For large amounts of data, you might want to consider exporting it from your Excel spreadsheet to an Access database. This is because Office products tend to work well together in this manner.

You may reformat the data to fit the rest of your spreadsheet and utilize it at your leisure once you have it. You should not post the information as your own (it does, after all, belong to someone else). When it comes to personal information, you must be even more cautious about utilizing information acquired from the internet. The norm is that anything important won't be easily available to you anyhow; however, like with any data source found on the internet, it's what you do with it that matters!

Excel's ability to extract text or data from a web page via a web query is helpful. Web sites frequently include relevant data that may be used to conduct further data analysis in Excel. Depending on your needs, you can receive refreshable data or retrieve data from a Web page and leave it static on your Excel worksheet. This piece will guide you through the steps of generating and running a web query in Microsoft Excel.

So, how can this possibly be useful? I'd be checking exchange rates daily, thus having the exchange rates, particularly for USD and GBP, automatically refresh regularly is a major plus.

Here's a small example to show how powerful this web query function in Excel can be.

• First, we must choose the cell in our worksheet to display the query's results. In my case, the findings will be presented in cell A1 on my worksheet.

• Select the Data Tab

• Get External Data Group

• Get Data From Web option

• New Web Query that displays a dialog box

Enter the website's URL or use the search box to find it.

Click the Go button

A yellow arrow will appear next to any available data tables.

A green check will appear next to the table after it has been selected.

After that, you may click the Import option.

Your spreadsheet will then display the specified data. Isn't it amazing?

As a result, we've automated the tedious job of copying currency rates from the Irish Times website. That's fine, but what else can we do with it? When you right-click on any of the cells that you've imported into your worksheet, you'll notice a few choices appear.

You may go ahead and choose Reload, which will refresh your query. If we select Data Range Properties, we will get a lot more choices.

I have the query configured to refresh each time I access the worksheet. My data will now be updated with the most recent exchange rates by accessing the Excel spreadsheet, saving me time from searching for the same information repeatedly.

Filter Results On Excel

A duplicate row in Excel is one where all data in cells match all data in another row. Duplicate values in cells are determined by the value displayed in the cell but not stored in the cell; for example, one cell with 01/02/2011 in it compared to February 01, 2011, is not duplicated but classed as unique values.

There a two ways to filter for unique values or remove unwanted information.

Both of these tasks are very similar and give the same results, one just hides the duplicate values (filtering), and the other deletes the duplicates permanently.

I suggest you conditionally format unique items in your Excel worksheet to ensure the results are what you expect before attempting to remove any of your data. This is a useful step which I always carry out and is easy in Excel 2007 onwards:

• Highlight the data set you want to search for duplicate items in

• Home Tab

• Styles Section

• Conditional Formatting

• Highlight Cell Rules

- Duplicate Values
- In the duplicate values dialog box, select how you want to highlight your cells with duplicate values
- Hit Ok

You can now easily see your duplicates before you attempt to temporarily filter or permanently delete them. To filter or temporarily remove duplicate values, we use the filter for the unique values function.

- Select the range of cells
- Data Tab
- Sort and Filter
- Advanced
- In the Advanced Filter Dialog Box
- Chose either Filter the list in place OR copy results to another location; in this case, you need to enter into the copy to box a cell reference or hide the dialog box and click into a cell on your worksheet, then select the expand dialog box

Your unique values will now be filtered either in place or to the location of your choosing.

If you choose to remove the duplicate values rather than just hide them by filtering, it is always good to make a copy of your data set as data will be permanently deleted from your worksheet.

To permanently delete duplicate data:

• Select the range of cells

• Data Tools Group

• Data Tab

• Click Remove Duplicates

• Under Columns, select one or more columns

• To quickly select all of your available columns, click Select All

• To quickly clear all of your available columns, click Unselect All

• Click Ok

• You will be notified by Excel how many duplicate values have been deleted

• You will also be notified by Excel how many unique values remain in your data set

• Click Ok

Not just numbers and formulae, but also language, are important data in Microsoft Excel. Excel has numerous options for improving text's style, look, and value, whether a column heading or a vital data piece.

Text Cell Formatting

One of the reasons you may be having trouble sorting or filtering data sets is because some data in a column is written as text while others are formatted as numbers. Numbers and punctuation will sort before the text in ascending sort order. If structured as a number, entries of 22, 1111, 33 would sort as 22, 333, 1111, and 1111, 22, 333 is represented as text (left-to-right).

When a variety of formats are used, the results will be inconsistent. The Text format is required for data with many places or leading zeros, such as 0001234.

One advantage of Excel is that you may format cells before entering data. This holds for both text and numbers. To format whole columns for text entry, select the column(s), then right-click and select Format Cells from the drop-down menu. Then, from the dialog box, select the Number tab, the Text format, and finally, OK. The Text alignment option is likewise available in Excel on the Ribbon's Home tab (Alignment group). For improved sorting and filtering results, apply the Text format to existing cells as well.

When Formatting Doesn't Go As Planned

Type an apostrophe (') in front of a single entry to convert it to text format.

Putting Two or More Cells Together (Sounds Like Cat)

It's possible that the data you already have isn't structured correctly. There are various options for displaying a full name for reporting, such as Last Name, First Name (Smith, Joe), and employee names in two columns, Last Name, and First Name. Column B is the last name, and Column C is the first name in the following instances. The formula to produce the Full Name in Column D is similar to (either example works):

=CONCATENATE(B2,",, "C2)<------ CONCATENATE is a "combination" function that includes additional text in quotations, such as the comma.

=B2 & ", " & C2<----- The & additionally adds the values from cells B2 and C2 together.

In Excel and Access, there's another use for the ampersand (&).

The ampersand (&) is a character used to merge or add several items in the example above.

Because the & is also part of special codes in Excel and Microsoft Access, a single ampersand will not function in most text entries (the output will be instead). In Excel or Access, use 2 ampersands, such as TIPS && TRICKS, to use an ampersand in a header, footer, or label. What a clever ruse!

Wrapping Text In Microsoft Excel, select the cells (or an entire row or column) for multiple line entries of labels, comments, notes, or descriptions, right-click on the selection and choose Format Cells, select the Alignment tab, and tick the option for Wrap Text, then OK. Wrap Text may also be accessed on the Ribbon's Home tab. The number of lines required to show the text is determined by the column width. For better readability, use this over several rows for long text entries and any data lists. You may further customize the layout by hitting [Alt] + [Enter] to force a line break or a new line within the same cell once the text has been prepared to allow wrapping.

To master text entering in Microsoft Excel, use these tips, techniques, and shortcuts.

Excel is a spreadsheet-creation program that you may use to organize your data. According to a recent study, it is the favored application for the great majority of enterprises worldwide. As a result, Excel has largely been used to create departmental budgets, expenditure reports, and various other accounting and financial outputs. Many long-time Excel users are unaware that the program comes with powerful database features built right in. The database aspect of Microsoft Excel will be revealed in this post.

It is critical to correctly arrange your data to fully utilize Excel's database functions. The column names are on the top row in the example below, with the data just beneath them in the subsequent rows. Always utilize consistent formatting for professional-looking databases/spreadsheets, such as the same styles for column labels.

Student# Last Name First Name Total Points
2123 Arellano Maria 170
2679 Black Michael 292
2680 Chase Tonia 280
1455 Davila Camilla 259
2681 Gabriel Maria 147
1270 Gonzales Juan 285
3245 Lopez Maria 252
1243 Miller Hailey 132
1454 Monaco Nicole 177
1878 Montoya Peter 150

When working with big spreadsheets with numerous rows of data, sorting and filtering the information might help you locate what you're searching for. When creating your lists, remember the following guidelines for successful sorting and filtering:

- Column labels must be in the first row or be beneath at least one blank row
- Data must be entered in contiguous rows and columns
- List data must be separated from other entries by at least one blank row or one blank column.
- Do not use duplicate field names
- Make a list of your records: Select all existing records and field names, then click Data in the Menu bar, point to List, click Create List, check the box next to My list has headers, and click OK.

You may use the Standard toolbar, the List toolbar, or the Data menu to organize records for quick viewing in a variety of ways:

Simple Sort: Sorts all of the items in a list according to a single field. Click buttons on the Standard toolbar with the current cell anywhere in the sort field column to arrange to ascend or descending order entries.

Custom Sort: Sort all records in a list according to up to three fields. Click the List button on the List toolbar and then choose Sort... with the current cell anywhere in the list, click the Data menu on the Menu bar, and select Sort... Make your selections in the dialog box, then click OK to proceed with the sort.

AutoFilter: When a range is configured as a List, arrows appear to the right of each field name. To temporarily filter out any records that do not satisfy one specific condition in one field (i.e., Level=Beginning 3), click the AutoFilter arrow for the field on which your criterion is based, and then click on the data you are looking for. Records that do not meet your requirement in the chosen field will be hidden until you click the AutoFilter arrow again and choose Show All.

Custom AutoFilter: If you want to base your filter on two criteria (for example, Level=Beginning 2 OR Level=Beginning 3), select (Custom...) from the AutoFilter menu. AND criteria can be used to define a record selection range.

Advanced Filter: Use an advanced filter if you want to base your filter on more than one or two criteria in more than one field and if you want to transfer the filtered data to another area in the workbook. The following steps are required for an advanced filter: 1) Make a criterion range using the field name(s) in question and insert the necessary criteria beneath the corresponding field name. 2) Determine where the results should be placed (be aware that any data directly below these destination cells may be erased); 3) Place the active cell anywhere in the data list; 4) Click the Data menu, point to Filter, and then click Advanced filter; 5) In the dialog box, specify the listed range, criteria range, and copy to range (be sure the Copy to another location option button is selected).

One of the quickest methods to arrange your data is to click once on a data-filled cell, i.e., any cell below the column labels, and then click the "Sort Ascending" or "Sort Descending" button on the Standard Toolbar. You may effectively alphabetize your data from A to Z or Z to A with a simple click of a button. After you've sorted the data, take a careful look at it. The records will retain their integrity; for example, if you sort in decreasing order, Peter Montoya, in our previous example, will rise to the top of the list, replete with his personal information, such as student number and total points.

Excel Autocorrect and Autofill

Auto Fill in Excel

With a few differences, AutoCorrect in Microsoft Excel is identical to AutoCorrect in Microsoft Word, whether you realize it or not. So, if you're not familiar with AutoCorrect, let me explain... AutoCorrect is a program that corrects the most frequent mistakes we make while we type. For example, if you enter 'cna' by accident, the AutoCorrect feature will transform the misspelled word to can. Why don't you try it for yourself? Take a look at what occurs when you type 'cna'.

The AutoCorrect Function, on the other hand, is considerably more than just an automatic word corrector or automated word spellchecker. It is a tool that can help you be more efficient at work. For example, if you were creating a paper or entering data into a spreadsheet and needed to insert a copyright symbol, you would most likely go to the Format menu, select the Symbol command from the drop-down menu, and select the Copyright symbol from the Symbols dialog box. What a ton of effort that was. Way too much work for me!

Microsoft has programmed the Autocorrect Function to write a few characters, and it will automatically insert the copyright sign, for example, type in (c). The copyright symbol should then appear. Other symbols, such as the Registered Trademark Symbol ® and the Trademark Symbol, are set up to operate similarly (TM). Simply type (r) to enter the registered trademark symbol and (t) to enter the Trademark Symbol (tm). As I'm sure you agree, understanding these few basic symbols may save you a lot of time, but the true power of Autocorrect lies in acronyms.

So, what exactly is an acronym?

In essence, an acronym is just a collection of letters that stand for a larger concept. In Australia, for example, we have two commercial terms: ABN and ACN. ABN and ACN are abbreviations for Australian Business Number and Australian Company Number, respectively. As you will certainly doubt note, if you had to spell out Australian Business Number and Australian Company Number every time you wanted to use those phrases, you would end up typing a ridiculous amount. So, using the AutoCorrect function, Microsoft has enabled you to encode these acronyms into AutoCorrect so that when you put them in, they will automatically convert to the complete phrase.

I'm aware, I'm aware, I'm aware. How do you manage it? So, here's what I'm going to tell you. The first step is to open Microsoft Excel, go to the Tools menu, and select the AutoCorrect Options function from the Tools menu.

The Autocorrect dialog box will appear in front of you, and if it is not already chosen, pick the Autocorrect tab. You'll notice a Check Box with the phrase, Replace as you Type, around halfway down the dialog box. This function corrects your spelling mistakes as you type; therefore, if the Check Box is not selected, AutoCorrect will not operate. From here, we'll input an acronym and have it return the entire text. For example, when I enter cjl, I want Autocorrect to replace it with my complete name, Christopher John Le Roy. First, I write in the acronym cjl in the Replace Text box, then in the With Text box, I simply enter my entire name, and finally, I choose the Add button and then the OK button to finish the procedure. You've just made your first Autocorrect entry.

Let's give it a go...

To test this, click in any cell, put in your acronym, and then press the spacebar. The acronym you wrote will become the text you typed in the With text box when you do this. If it didn't work, make sure you chose the Replace as you Type command in the Autocorrect dialog box.

An autoCorrect is a great tool that, when used correctly, can save you hours of effort and heartache with acronyms. The amazing thing about AutoCorrect in Microsoft Excel is that once you install an AutoCorrect function in Microsoft Excel, it becomes available in other programs such as Microsoft Word, Microsoft PowerPoint, and many other Microsoft Office products.

You can save time and patience by using the Autofill options in Excel to allow you to format and enter data into multiple cells in a worksheet. With these functions, you can copy a piece of data into a range of cells, copy the format from one cell into the range or complete a series (e.g., 1, 2, 3, etc.).

Starting in one cell (we'll call it the "master"), type a number, and then move the mouse over the bottom right-hand corner; a plus sign appears. A small menu icon is displayed at the bottom right-hand corner of the last selected cell. This menu gives access to the options.

The copy option is the default action that Excel performs when you click and drag, so you should notice that the number you entered into the master cell has been copied into all of the cells you selected. To change the default action to the fill series function, click on the menu icon and select 'Fill Series.' You can also fill a series across a row (click on the + sign and drag from left to right instead of downwards), or you can fill backward (3, 2, 1, etc.) by clicking and dragging upwards or from right to left.

If you want to create a row or column with identical formatting without carrying across the data, you can choose the 'Fill Formatting Only option. Alternatively, you can opt to fill without formatting. Note, however, that if the master cell contains specific formatting before it is selected and you opt to fill a series, the formatting will always be copied across; or if you opt to fill without formatting, the fill a series function will not be actioned. The best way to fill a series without copying the formatting is to leave the master cell unformatted, fill the series and then select and format the required cells.

AutoCorrect will:

Correct frequent typing mistakes like using "teh" instead of "the" and capitalizing the initial letter of each day of the week. As a result, "Monday" becomes "Monday."

The initial letter of each phrase should be capitalized.

Correct improper Caps Lock key usage, such as "sHOULD."

Two beginning capitals, such as "SHould," should be corrected.

These choices can be tailored to meet your specific needs.

To access the AutoCorrect Options, press the following keys:

Click Tools > AutoCorrect Options

Select Office > Word Options > Proofing > AutoCorrect Options from the Office menu.

Click Ok after checking or unchecking the appropriate items.

Add an AutoCorrect Entry

You have the option of adding a new entry to the AutoCorrect dictionary. This is an excellent feature to employ to boost your productivity. It may considerably speed up data entry while also reducing spelling errors.

When you add a new item or modify the AutoCorrect settings in Word, it is updated across all Microsoft Office programs, making it easier to work in Excel and Outlook.

Let's assume I want to add a definition for Microsoft Office training. When I type mso into a Word document or an Excel spreadsheet, the content is replaced by Microsoft Office training.

1. When you need to input the text mso, this comes in useful. It might be an acronym, someone's initials, or the name of a project or company.

2. Enter mso in the Replace: box

3. Enter Microsoft Office training in the With box

4. Click Ok

5. Click Ok again

When you type mso into an Office program, the text gets substituted by Microsoft Office training.

Preventing Text Replacement Automatically

A blue line appears below the first letter of the first word input when Word changes the text. If you move your cursor over this blue line, a smart tag will display with AutoCorrect Options.

This tag lets you prevent Word from updating the mso automatically. When you need to input the text mso, this comes in useful. It might be an acronym, someone's initials, or the name of a project or company.

Select either Change back to "mso" or Stop Automatically Correcting "mso" by clicking the AutoCorrect Options smart tag.

This is beneficial, but it is inefficient. When using AutoCorrect, a helpful tip is to precede the word to be substituted with a symbol. Instead of mso, for example, we might have used /mso or?mso.

Using a consistent prefix for all of your custom AutoCorrect entries prevents the possibility of AutoCorrect mistakingly substituting the word mso with Microsoft Office training in the future.

Removing an AutoCorrect Entry

To remove an entry:

1. Open AutoCorrect Options

2. In the Replace: box, type the first few letters of the word and choose it from the list.

3. Click Delete

Enable/Disable AutoComplete in Excel

The procedures to enable or disable AutoComplete in Microsoft Excel vary by version:

IN EXCEL 2019, 2016, 2013, AND 2010

1. Navigate to the File > Options menu.

2. In the Excel Options window, open Advanced on the left.

3. Toggle Enable AutoComplete for cell values on or off under the Editing

Options section, depending on whether you wish to enable or deactivate this function.

1. Click or tap OK to save the changes and continue using Excel.

IN EXCEL 2007

1. Click the Office Button.

2. Choose Excel Options to bring up the Excel Options dialog box.

3. Choose Advanced in the pane to the left.

4. Click the box next to the Enable AutoComplete for cell values option box to turn this feature on or off.

5. Choose OK to close the dialog box and return to the worksheet.

IN EXCEL

1. Navigate to Tools > Options from the menu bar to open the Options dialog box.

2. Choose the Edit tab.

3. Toggle AutoComplete on/off with the checkmark box next to the Enable AutoComplete for cell values option.

4. On the Save Changes page, click OK.

When to Use AutoComplete and When Not to Use It

When putting data into a spreadsheet with a lot of duplicates, AutoComplete comes in handy. When you turn on AutoComplete, it will auto-fill the rest of the information from the context surrounding it, allowing you to enter data faster.

Let's say you're filling in numerous cells with the same name, location, or other information. If you didn't have AutoComplete, you'd have to retype the data or copy and paste it again and over, which wastes time.

For example, if you entered "Mary Washington" in the first cell and then "George" and "Harry" in the following ones, you may input "Mary Washington" again much faster by entering "M" and then clicking Enter, and Excel will auto-type the entire name.

This works with any amount of text entries in any cell in any series, so you could write "H" at the bottom to have Excel suggest "Harry," and then type "M" again if you require that name auto-completed. No data has to be copied or pasted.

AutoComplete, on the other hand, isn't necessarily your best buddy. Even if you don't need to repeat anything, it will auto-suggest it every time you start entering something with the same initial letter as the prior data, which might be more hassle than a benefit.

9. MICROSOFT EXCEL SKILLS TO KNOW WHEN JOB HUNTING

Job seekers or career changers have probably noticed that many professions require computer skills. The exact amount of the required abilities may vary greatly depending on the sort of work you seek. Still, even the most basic occupations that put you in front of a computer will require some understanding of Microsoft Excel.

However, if you are inexperienced with the software, this employment need should not be a complete impediment. Even if you've never used Microsoft Excel, you may use this book to learn what you need to know to apply for jobs that need it.

Acquaint yourself with the Excel interface and terminology.

Companies tend to postpone system updates or upgrades until a problem arises; therefore, it may surprise you to hear that many organizations still use Microsoft Excel 2003. Since then, there have been numerous full version updates, but Excel 2003 still maintains a sizable fan base and install base.

As a result, while applying for a position, you may be required to be familiar with various versions of Excel. However, regardless of whatever version of Microsoft Excel you are using (new versions are produced every few years and are recognized by the year of release), A few things will always remain the same, regardless of whatever version of Microsoft Excel you use (for example, Microsoft Excel 2010, Microsoft Excel 2013, or Microsoft Excel 2016). A pattern of small rectangles will fill the Excel window. These rectangles are called cells and are organized in rows and columns. Columns are made up of cells arranged vertically; rows are made up of cells arranged horizontally.

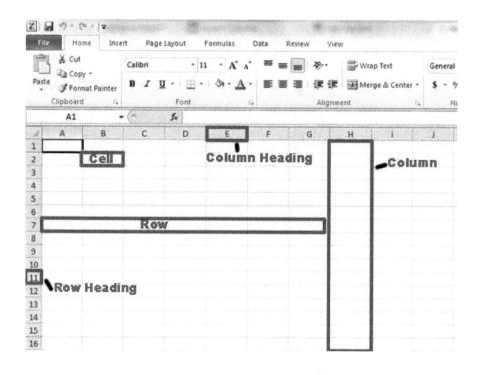

When you click on one of the cells, you can input a number or letter, and the result will be presented in the cell. The information in the cell is referred to as the value. You may rearrange, sort, and modify the appearance of your cells and values by selecting one of the choices at the top of the screen.

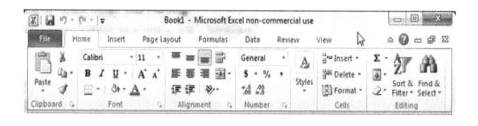

The look of the menus will alter based on the version of Excel you are using, and regrettably, many different firms utilize various versions of the application. As long as you know what you're trying to do, you should be able to find the right menu item in each iteration of the game.

Excel Sorting Tasks You Should Know For Job Searching

If you are given a pre-hire competence assessment, you will most likely be given a random collection of data that you must arrange. Sorting a series of cells in Excel is a frequent task in your new job. Excel allows you to alphabetize a list of last names or order a sequence of numbers from highest to lowest with a single click of a button. Furthermore, the process for sorting words and numbers is the same, and you have the option of sorting from lowest to highest or highest to lowest.

Another method for sorting your data is to copy and paste information from its current cell to where you need it. If you've ever used a copy and paste feature in another application, the one in Excel is the same. Click a cell, then press Ctrl + C on your keyboard to copy it (or Ctrl + X to cut it), then click the appropriate destination cell and hit Ctrl + V on your keyboard to paste it.

This method may also be used to duplicate a whole row, column, or group of cells. Then use the copy and paste techniques mentioned earlier to highlight your selected cells.

A last technique of sorting is to use Excel's Hide and Unhide options. This allows you to hide a row or column from the display without removing the corresponding range of data from the spreadsheet. Hide the row number or column letter by selecting it using the right-click menu. Unhide a row or column by choosing the rows or columns before and after the hidden series, right-clicking, and selecting Unhide.

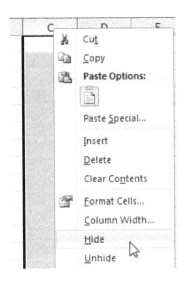

Excel Display Formatting Options That Are Beneficial

Another category of Excel activities that you may regularly encounter centers on modifying the appearance and printing of your cells. You may change the color of your cells, the look of the font, and the size of your cells in each version of Excel. Color changes may be made easily in all versions of Excel by right-clicking the cell and selecting one of the formatting choices from the shortcut menu.

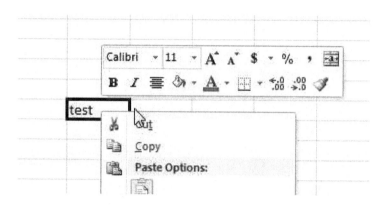

Right-click on the row number or column name and pick row height or column width. If you pick a group of rows or columns, the same function is used.

The Page Setup menu provides the last option for formatting the look of your Excel file, particularly for printing. Click the Page Setup button in the bottom-right corner of the Page Setup section on the Page Layout menu to access the Page Setup menu.

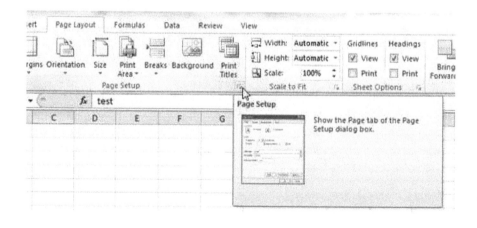

This menu lets you choose the orientation of your page, page margins, header information, and whether or not gridlines should be printed on the page. Printing gridlines is an extremely important factor when printing Excel files since it provides the best method for making a printed document more legible. Unless otherwise told, I generally include these by default.

Some Excel Basic Calculations and Formulas

The most common issue I see with Excel files is simply putting many numbers together. Especially in commercial environments, where many orders and reports may be large spreadsheets, including columns that must be combined to determine the total value. I've seen individuals manually put values in Excel together, which nearly negates the point of the software. Excel has an AutoSum button on the Formulas bar that sums a sequence of numbers for you. Click the AutoSum button, choose the cells to be added together, and then click Enter. The sum of the cell totals will be presented in the first cell underneath or to the right of the cells you chose.

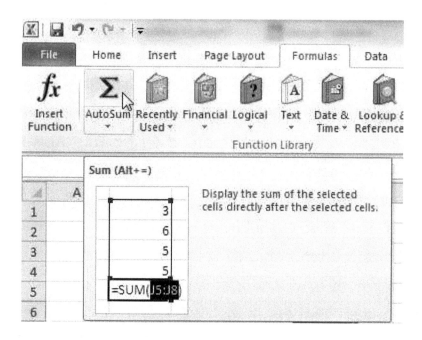

You may also enter formulae into cells to have a greater say over where the total is presented. Formulas are generally written in the form =A1+A2, =A1-A2, =A1*A2 or =A1/A2. If you're intrigued, you can write an AutoSum function by hand using the format =SUM (A1:A2).

Practice, Practice, and More Practice

Excel, like nearly everything else in life, requires practice to improve. You may execute certain activities with guidance. Still, your true worth to a potential employer will emerge when you can complete any of these duties smoothly from memory. This will enhance your production, which will raise your worth. Furthermore, as you continue to use Excel, you will discover new approaches to do jobs. You will also discover additional useful tips and methods for quickly organizing, sorting, and manipulating huge volumes of data.

If you're just starting in the job market or wanting to change careers, you've undoubtedly noticed that many of the available positions demand some level of computer knowledge. The exact amount of the required abilities may vary greatly depending on the sort of work you seek. Still, even the most basic occupations that need you to sit in front of a computer will require some understanding of Microsoft Excel. However, this job need should not be a total obstacle if you are inexperienced with the program. You may use this section to understand what you need to know about Microsoft Excel before applying for jobs that need it.

Become acquainted with the Excel interface and terminology.

Many organizations still use Microsoft Excel 2003, which may surprise you. Companies have a propensity to wait until an issue arises before making adjustments or updates to their system. Since then, there have been two complete version upgrades, yet Excel still has a sizable user base. So, while applying for a job, you may need to know multiple Excel versions. However, regardless of whatever version of Microsoft Excel you're using (new versions are produced every few years and are recognized by their release year), A few items will always remain the same in Microsoft Excel 2010 (for example). A pattern of tiny rectangles covers the bulk of the Excel display. Each of these rectangles represents a cell, which is arranged into rows and columns. A row is a horizontal succession of cells, whereas a column is a vertical sequence of cells.

When you click on one of the cells, you may input a number or letter appearing in the cell. The value is the information in the cell.

Using the options at the top of the screen, you may arrange, sort, and change the look of your cells and values.

The menus will look different depending on the version of Excel you're using, and many different organizations, regrettably, utilize various versions of the application. However, the most fundamental functionality is there in each iteration, so as long as you know what you need to accomplish, you should be able to find the appropriate menu option.

Excel Sorting Tasks to Be Aware Of While Job Hunting

One of the most typical jobs you'll need to know while using Excel in your new profession is sorting a sequence of cells. If you take a pre-hire competency exam, you may be given a random collection of facts that you must arrange. Excel allows you to alphabetize a list of last names or order a sequence of numbers from highest to lowest with a single click of a button. Words and numbers can also be sorted in the same way, from lowest to highest or vice versa.

Another option for sorting your data is to copy and paste information from its current cell to the area where you truly need it. If you've ever used a copy and paste feature in another software, you'll know how to utilize the one in Excel. To paste, select a cell and press Ctrl + C (or Ctrl + X to cut it), then select the desired destination cell and press Ctrl + V. If you wish to copy a whole row, column, or group of cells, use this method. Select your preferred cells by clicking the row number on the left side of the window, the column letter on the top of the window, or by using your mouse to highlight them, then use the copy and paste procedures described previously.

The Hide and Unhide options in Excel provide the last choice for sorting. This allows you to hide a row or column from view while keeping the data in the spreadsheet intact. You may conceal a row or column by right-clicking the row number or column letter, then selecting Conceal. To reveal a hidden row or column, pick the rows or columns immediately before and follow the hidden series using your mouse.

Excel Formatting Options for Display

Adjusting the appearance of your cells and the way they print is another set of Excel chores that you'll experience regularly. You may change the color of your cells, the font's look, and the size of your cells in each version of Excel. In all versions of Excel, you can rapidly change the color of a cell by right-clicking it and selecting from the formatting choices in the shortcut menu.

You may change the size of a row or column by right-clicking it and selecting the row height or column width option. If you choose a collection of rows or columns, the same function applies.

The Page Setup menu provides the last option for formatting the look of your Excel file, particularly for printing. The Page Setup menu may be accessed by clicking the Page Setup button in the Page Setup section of the Page Layout menu's bottom-right corner.

This menu allows you to define the page's orientation, margins, header information, and whether or not to print gridlines on the page. Creating gridlines is a significant consideration when printing Excel files since it gives the best technique for making a printed document more legible. I typically include these by default unless expressly asked not to.

Some Excel Formulas and Basic Calculations

Adding a bunch of numbers together is the most typical problem I run into with Excel files. This is especially true in commercial situations where many orders and reports are large spreadsheets with columns that must be put together to establish the entire worth of a sale. I've personally witnessed individuals manually combining values in Excel, which virtually contradicts the program's purpose. Excel has an AutoSum button on the Formulas bar that will automatically sum a sequence of numbers for you. Using the AutoSum button, choose the cells you wish to combine, then press Enter. The sum of the cells is shown in the first cell underneath or to the right of the cells you chose.

For a bit more flexibility over where the total is shown, you may type formulae into cells. Formulas are usually written in the following format: =A1+A2, =A1-A2, =A1*A2, or =A1/A2. You may manually write an AutoSum function using the format =SUM if you're intrigued (A1:A2).

Perfection comes with practice.

Excel, like nearly everything else in life, requires practice to improve. You may be able to complete particular activities with guidance. Still, your true worth to a potential employer will be demonstrated when you can accomplish any of these duties flawlessly from memory. As a consequence, your production will rise, and your worth will rise as well. Furthermore, as you continue to use Excel, you will learn new ways to perform tasks and pick up new tips and tricks that will make organizing, sorting, and manipulating large amounts of data in seconds much easier.

Workbooks in Excel

A Microsoft Excel file collects worksheets, charts, graphs, and other relevant Excel objects into a single location. Workbooks come in various shapes and sizes, depending on the version of Microsoft Excel you're using. Each workbook has a distinct purpose that distinguishes it from the others.

What Are the Different Components of a Workbook?

Worksheets, which Excel users can use to store, edit, and manipulate data, charts, and graphs, which Excel users can use to display their data in a variety of customizable ways, and macros, which Excel users can use to create or record custom commands to fit their specific needs, are just a few of the components.

What Characteristics Does a Workbook Possess?

They include various functions, including the ability to create, rename, and modify numerous spreadsheets, charts, and graphs. They also give users the option of storing custom menus and instructions within each worksheet. Excel users may modify an Excel workbook in various ways using some of the most common features, such as macros, the ribbon, and the quick access toolbar.

What Are Workbook Tools Available?

Within Excel spreadsheets, users have access to a variety of essential features. Users may modify virtually any property using tools like the file menu and backstage view. Users may generate easy-to-access pictures of critical portions of their workbook using tools like custom views and frozen panes. Users can transmit and receive data from a variety of workbook-related sites using tools like exporting and importing.

What are the different kinds of Excel Workbooks?

There are several varieties of workbooks and numerous ways to export workbooks to other file formats. There are just too many varieties to discuss here. But I'll make an exception. For a good reason, the Excel Workbook is one of the most widely used workbooks. This worksheet can be opened in most versions of Excel by Excel users.

Is it possible to protect my workbook?

Yes, you can secure a workbook in Excel in a few different ways. Password encryption and worksheet and workbook protection are just a few features that help users secure their workbooks. Other users won't be able to quickly modify the appearance and format of your workbook if you utilize tools like concealing worksheets and marking it as final. Depending on the situation, users can construct custom views and freeze panes to show or conceal particular views. These are especially useful when your workbooks get larger, and you need to condense material in various ways.

10. HOW TO EXPORT A CHART FROM MICROSOFT EXCEL TO MICROSOFT POWERPOINT

Excel is a spreadsheet application that is both sophisticated and simple to use. Excel charts may be used to visually communicate complicated data to people in a variety of situations. Excel 2010 adds a slew of new chart-making capabilities. When you only want to show the audience the Excel chart and not the whole dataset, the Microsoft PowerPoint program may be the best option. While PowerPoint has its own set of charting tools, drawing the charts in the PowerPoint slide that are already in the Excel workbook would be extremely complex and time-consuming. As a result, exporting the charts from Excel to PowerPoint or importing the charts from Excel to PowerPoint would be a sensible option. In any case, you will save a significant amount of time and work.

Copy and paste the Excel chart into a PowerPoint slide. Follow the steps below to do this:

• Open the Excel file with the Excel chart in it. Select the chart from the specific sheet.

• Select Copy from the Clipboard group on the Home tab and click it.

- You may also hold down the CTRL and C buttons at the same time.

• A copy of the graph is saved to the clipboard. Now it's time to look at the PowerPoint presentation.

• Select the slide where you wish to paste the chart in the PowerPoint presentation.

• Select Paste from the Clipboard group on the Home tab and click it.

- To activate the keyboard shortcut, press CTRL + V.

- The graph will be copied and pasted into the PowerPoint slide.

• At the bottom of the pasted chart, a tiny set of Paste Option icons will appear. There are several alternatives available; select the most appropriate one for your needs.

• The chart should be connected to the source data to maintain the PowerPoint slide data consistent with the Excel workbook data. Select the option "Chart (connected to Excel data)" in the PowerPoint program to link the chart in the PowerPoint slide to the Excel workbook. Choose the 'Paste as Picture' option to display the chart as a static picture. Preserve Source Formatting if you want to keep the original format. Alternatively, you can paste and format the chart using the destination theme by selecting the Use Destination Theme option.

• To modify the chart's appearance, go to the design tab and select the style form from the chart styles option.

• The Picture format may be used to see the chart as a stationary picture, and it produces a higher-quality image than the usual Bitmap format.

Charts from an existing Excel workbook can be inserted. The graphic does not need to be recreated in the PowerPoint presentation. It's possible to import it from an Excel spreadsheet. The following are the steps to take:

• Go to the slide in the PowerPoint presentation where you want to put the chart.

• After you've activated the slide, go to the Insert tab and click on the Object button in the Text group.

• Select the Create New button to start a new chart. Choose MS Office Excel Chart, for example, to create a new excel chart.

• To enter a chart already in an excel worksheet, select Create from file and then click OK.

• Go to the chart's position in the file using the Browse button. After you've selected the file, click OK.

• If you need to maintain a connection to the source file, click the link box. Then press the OK button.

• The chart can be shown as an icon without being pasted. To do so, tick the box labeled "Display as icon" and then click OK.

• On the slide, there will be an icon of an excel workbook. Drag it to the location you want it to be.

• If required, resize and place the chart in the source file. The first of the two procedures is superior to the other. You may learn more about the methods by looking through the help files that come with the Excel software. For more detailed information, you might wish to chat with an Excel professional. There are numerous methods and tips, and techniques for various jobs in various versions of Microsoft applications on the internet. Visit the site and select the program associated with your issue, then look for the needed topics. This will undoubtedly assist you in resolving your issue.

How to Make a Database in Microsoft Excel

Because my primary role in the IT business has been database creation, and the spreadsheeting community's primary tool is what I consider an overly complicated list, the term "Microsoft Excel Database" has never sat well with me. However, for the sake of peace, I'd like to lay down some of the guidelines you must follow while creating a Microsoft Excel database.

Let's have a look...

In essence, a database is a collection of information that is linked together in some way. For example, if you were operating a business and selling a product, you may create a database that records all of the sales you've made over time. Storing this information in a database would make sense because corporate information and product sales are linked and would be acceptable for a database.

There are many various types of databases, such as Microsoft Access databases, Oracle databases, MySQL databases, etc. However, Microsoft Excel offers a database list feature. The list's format is nearly identical to that of other databases, with data organized by column headings in rows; however, after that common point, the Excel database diverges. To find particular data in a Microsoft Excel Database or Excel List, we utilize specifically designed functions rather than the conventional database language of SQL. Criteria are custom-written functions that you create yourself.

So, how do we make a database in Excel...

First and foremost, there is one guideline that we must always adhere to one excel database per worksheet. Any longer, and you'll find yourself in a lot of trouble. Create a separate worksheet for each database if you require several excel databases in your workbook.

The second thing to know is that your database list's header must be on the first row. Your field names are listed in the first row. Furthermore, each field name must be unique. You can't have two field names that are the same; otherwise, you'll end up with a useless list.

The next problem you'll have to deal with is determining the field names. The field or column names in Excel databases must be unique, according to a simple criterion. To finish, make sure the field names are distinct from the rest of the database in terms of data types, format, and pattern. To comply with this rule, I usually style my field names in bold.

One of the essential principles to follow when creating an excel database is that there must be a blank row and column surrounding the fields and data. This means that while a heading can be placed at the top of the fields, a blank row between the header and the fields and along the last column is required. The rule of the blank row likewise applies at the bottom of the list.

When adding data into your list, each record must have the same amount of fields, and each cell in each record must have some value, even if it is just blank (a blank value is still considered a value). If a field doesn't have any data, leave it blank and go on to the next one.

When putting data into a field, be sure there are no gaps between the text and the field's conclusion. If there are spaces in the list, sorting and searching for data will be hampered, and you will obtain surprising results.

Unless you expressly inform the Microsoft Excel program that upper and lower case characters in the field influence searches or sort orders, upper and lower case characters do not affect searches or sort orders. If necessary, you may also utilize formulae in a cell. Formulas can refer to cells both inside and outside of the Excel Database List.

You may also update and format the cells just like any other spreadsheet, but the most important thing to remember is that the field names must be formatted differently than the rest of the data in the database list. Except for the field headers, it is strongly advised that the list has no further styling. This prevents the program from erroneously determining what is and is not a field header in the excel database.

Now that you've built up your list according to these principles, you're ready to query it using criteria. The Form dialog box is the simplest method to accomplish this. Select the Data menu and then Form from the drop-down menu to enter the Excel Database form.

Choose the Criteria button on the Excel Database Form, input the requirements you have for your data, and then select the Find Next button to be sent to the first entry that meets your criteria. Excel databases are very beneficial for summary data, or when the number of rows in your database does not exceed 65,536 rows.

If you follow these guidelines while creating an excel database, the functions connected with the excel database list will be effective and efficient.

11. THE MANY SHAPES OF THE MOUSE POINTER

I come across many people whose line of work necessitates some basic level of numeric computations or the entry of a series of numbers and values. Still, due to a lack of knowledge, they do the simplest of these activities with great difficulty and drain their daily productivity.

The Microsoft Excel Spreadsheet, often known as Excel, is the favored choice for numerical-based computations with almost no limit to the number of results obtained.

Other spreadsheet software exists, but this section is intended to help novices become familiar with the fundamental features and ideas of Microsoft Excel, the most powerful and frequently used spreadsheet of all time.

The Mouse Pointer's Various Shapes

People frequently have trouble working with Excel because they don't comprehend the various forms of the mouse cursor on spreadsheet events. Understanding the shifting forms of the mouse pointer is a step forward in getting things done properly and swiftly while performing any important computation.

The fact that there are no descriptions for the forms of the mouse pointers as they change during activities is bad for novice users.

The Excel Cells

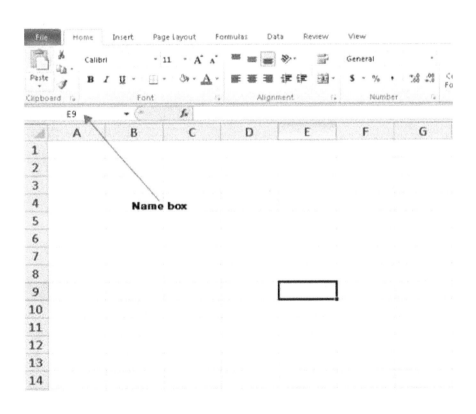

Name box

Excel, unlike other spreadsheets, is built using cells as the consequence of rows and columns; notice how the column letters start horizontally at 'A' and go on indefinitely?

Similarly, the rows that increase the vertical size of the worksheet are labeled sequentially from '1' to over a million rows. The length of the spreadsheet gives the impression that the rows and columns are limitless, although they are, in fact, finite. The spreadsheet is so time-consuming that it's virtually unquantifiable.

In most workbooks, each cell is automatically scaled by default. You'll likely need to resize the cells to meet your needs. Hover the mouse over the division lines across the cell's column letter or row number. Note how the mouse cursor changes to the re-size bar (vertical resizer when on the row, horizontal resizer when on the column row), and drag.

The Fill Handle And The Active Cell

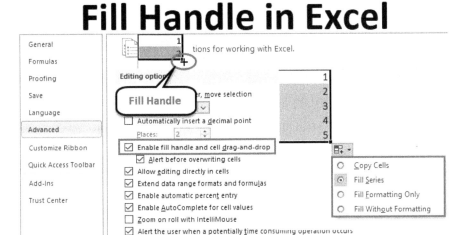

At any given time, only one active cell can exist. The active cell in a spreadsheet is the one that is open for data entry. The active cell has a strong black border, and its address is shown in the name field. The number of the row and the letter of the column are also highlighted.

When you click on a cell in a spreadsheet, it becomes active. Notice the tiny square in the thick black border's bottom right-hand corner? The fill handle is what it's called. You may use the fill handle to duplicate the contents of an active cell to nearby cells by gently dragging outside the fill handle of the beginning cell to extend to a series of cells to fill to the destination cell. (Notice how the cursor transforms from a large white cross to a little black cross.) When it comes to incrementing numbers from a starting cell, the fill handle is quite useful.

The fill handle eliminates the need to type the months of the year or the days of the week. For example, if the first cell includes months like January or March or any other day of the week, the fill handle will automatically increase successive entries until the required time is reached.

The Name-Box in Excel

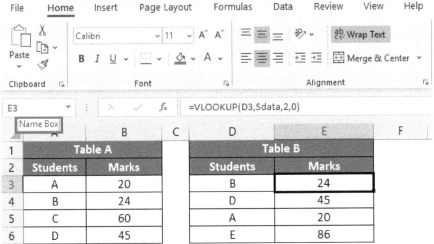

Because Excel is made up of rows and columns, each cell in the spreadsheet is individually recognized by a row/column name. "Cell columnA Row1" or "Cell A1" would be a unique designation for the first cell in the top-left corner of the Excel page, for example.

With this knowledge, each cell in the spreadsheet is connected to a row and column that uniquely identifies the cell in question, and the name box, which shows the name of each reference cell, saves the user from having to count or figure out the location of each cell at any given moment.

The name box's principal role is to display the name of the reference cells or an active cell at any given moment.

Option to Select All Cells

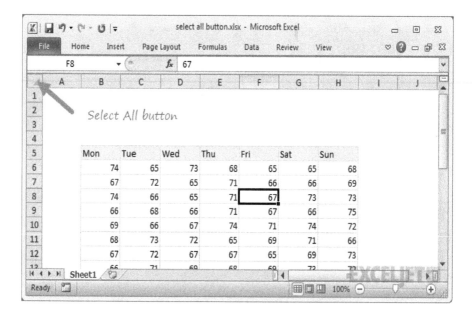

Just below the name field, Microsoft Excel gives a small triangle button representing the top left junction of the row and column. This button selects all cells in the same way as "Ctrl +A" does.

The Formula in Excel

| SUM | ⇕ | ✕ | ✓ | *fx* | =SUM(B2, C2) |

	A	B	C	D
1	Source of Leads	November Leads	December Leads	Total Leads
2	Blog Post 1	10	15	=SUM(B2, C2)
3	Blog Post 2	4	12	
4	Blog Post 3	11	7	
5	Blog Post 4	2	8	
6	Blog Post 5	12	19	
7	Blog Post 6	6	11	
8	Blog Post 7	8	8	
9	Blog Post 8	17	19	
10	Blog Post 9	3	6	
11	Blog Post 10	8	14	
12				

The amazing capabilities of Excel's functioning are due to formulas. If you write formulas correctly, you can get results for almost any degree of computation you can think of. The use of a formula is the most common method of performing simple computations.

Excel's architecture demands that computations be conducted on cell references rather than values or cell content directly. We may go like "5+6" on a traditional spreadsheet, but with Excel, you'll get something like "=B2 + C2," where B2 refers to 5 and C2 refers to 6.

Advanced users can enter formulas directly into the formula bar, referencing the effective cells rather than typing them in the cells.

Basic principles apply while writing a formula. The equal symbol "=" is always used to begin a formula. The equal sign turns on the formulae that can handle your request. All conventional mathematical operations, such as addition, subtraction, and division, apply when creating formulae.

Every Excel formula should be typed using brackets, and Excel will automatically compute and show the results in the same cell where the formula was input. (The findings will overwrite your computed formula.) The formula bar, which is adjacent to the name box, will display your formula.

Basic formulas include =sum(A2:B2), =sum(A2+B2), =sum(A2*B2), and =sum(A2/B2).

The colon is preferable when doing addition in Excel over the addition sign, especially when working with numerous cells.

Below are some examples of formulae.

To determine the sum of a sequence of integers, use SUM ().

The function AVERAGE() is used to calculate the average of a set of integers.

MAX() is a function that finds the highest value in a set of numbers.

The MIN() function is used to determine the lowest value in a collection of integers.

TODAY() is used to display the current date.

Format for Data Entry

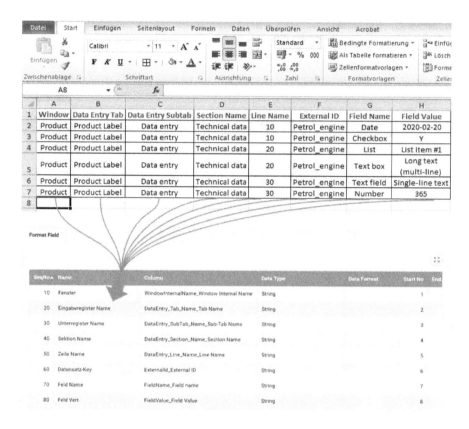

Excel detects dates, currency, text, and numbers in the spreadsheet automatically. Understanding how Excel handles these various data kinds can aid you in organizing your work as effectively as possible.

The majority of individuals are unaware that Excel aligns numbers or currencies to the right and texts to the left of the cell. Mixing words and numbers in a single cell can be dangerous since it defeats the purpose of numeric computation. Excel will align these combined words and numbers to the left, preventing you from using a formula for computation or, at worst, displaying incorrect results.

For most users, data input is a difficult task. When importing data into Excel from external sources, Excel may misinterpret the numbers as text, making computations difficult. The secret to overcoming this easy but perplexing problem is to highlight the cells that need to be changed and then pick Numbers from the Number format drop-down menu on the home ribbon. The format is set to General by default.

Cells of Relatives

Cell Reference in Excel

	I2		fx	=G2*H2		G2		fx	=SUMIFS($C$2:$C$17,$A$2: $A$17,$F2,$B$2:$B$17,G$1)
	F	G	H			F	G	H	I
1	Product	Unit Price	Its Sold	S	1	Sales Manager	Jan	Feb	Mar
2	Product **Relative Cell**		20	3	2	Manisha **Mixed Cell**		9,965.00	53,728.00
3	Product **Reference**		21	10	3	Shalu **Reference**		4,994.00	76,055.00
4	Product		2		4	Neelika		3,145.00	63,099.00
5	Product-4	2,956.00	22	6	5	Ruchi	89,685.00	15,164.00	31,152.00
6	Product-5	5,956.00	23	13					
7	Product-6	6,956.00	24	16		C1		fx	=$A$1
8	Product-7	7,956.00	1					D	E
9	Product-8	8,956.00	7	6		**Absolute Cell**		5	5
10	Product-9	9,956.00	10	9	1	**Reference**	5		
11	Product-10	1,056.00	11	1	2				
12					3				

All cell references in the worksheet are relative cells by default. When you move the fill handle outside a cell, the formulae or words will alter depending on the relative location of the rows and columns.

If you move the =sum(A1+B1) formula from row 1 to rows 2 and 3, it becomes =sum(A2+B2) and =sum(A3+B3), respectively. The reference to the rows is altered about the row number, whereas ColumnA is retained.

Using relative cells, numbers, dates, days, years, weeks, values, and other items can all be incremented. When you repeat the first cell in any of these instances, the cells are automatically filled with the right data.

12. DISPLAY FORMULAS ON EXCEL

Excel's ability to modify complicated formulae is one of its most valuable features. Excel includes several built-in functions that make it easier to perform various actions on the data in your spreadsheets. Whether you utilize Excel's built-in functions or create your own, you may need to modify a formula. Excel 2007 makes it very simple to edit formulae, and it has built-in support to help you manage complex formulas.

A current formula can be changed in any way you wish. Double-click the cell that contains the formula to be changed in Excel 2007 to begin modifying it. The formula's contents will appear in the formula bar, which is located directly above the worksheet.

If you want to change the value of a referred cell or range, double-click the reference in the formula bar. In the actual worksheet, Excel 2007 will highlight the relevant cell or group of cells. Select the new reference cell by clicking on it. The new reference cell will be automatically inserted into the formula at the proper location by Excel 2007. To close the cell, type enter.

A reference range of cells can also be replaced. Double-click the first cell in the range and drag your mouse to highlight the second cell to replace it in the formula bar. From within the spreadsheet, click and drag the replacement range. The new range will take the place of the old one in Excel. To close the cell, press enter.

When utilizing these ways to alter formulae in Excel 2007, avoid clicking any unnecessary cells since Excel 2007 will put them into your formula. If you've added a cell by mistake (or just picked the wrong cell) and haven't yet clicked Enter to close it, use Esc instead. This will depart the cell without the erroneous modifications you've made being accepted. Start again by highlighting the cell. Select the cell and re-edit it if you've already accepted the changes.

It's very simple to change formulae directly in Excel 2007. Place your mouse in the appropriate spot in the formula bar and start typing. You may use this method to add, remove, or change any part of the formula. To accept the changes, hit Enter once you've done editing. To prevent introducing mistakes, make sure to maintain any essential parenthesis and double-check for typographical errors before closing the cell.

One of the most important text formulae to have in your Excel toolbox is the LEN formula. It returns the length of a text string after counting the characters in it.

The formula's syntax is =LEN (text)

So, how would you put this method to work for you? When migrating from one database to another, I utilized it to detect issues with the length of database fields. The address line column in my previous database was not constrained and could contain up to 255 characters. Because the address column in my new database is now limited to 30 characters, I needed to discover any issues with the data import before it took place. The LEN function in Excel was used to do this. Here's how to do it:

• Open the Excel file containing the data export (in my instance, an address table).

• Add a column to the right of Column C to contain the results of the LEN calculation; in this example, I added a column to the right of Column C to hold my address data.

• Insert Function or pick the first cell in the column and hit = to begin the formula

• The Formula tab, To begin the formula, insert a function or choose the first cell in the column and press =.

• Click the cell where you want to determine the string length (in this case, column B)

• Select LEN or type LEN in the open brackets (

If you use the formula wizard, Excel will show you the solution right away, or you may close the brackets and press OK to complete inputting the formula manually.

We only need to duplicate the formula along the full column now:

• Use your mouse to scroll down the column and SHIFT-click in the last cell.

• Press Ctrl+D

We now know the character count of column B, which is now displayed in column C. Let's go ahead and highlight any of the character count cells that are over 30 characters with conditional formatting.

• Select Column C cells

• Home Tab- Style Group

• Conditional Formatting

• Highlight Cell Rules

• Select Great Than- we're searching for cells with more than 30 characters, so enter 30 and choose the kind of formatting- I'll leave it as the default display.

• Hit OK

You have it; all of the cells that will create issues have been marked and addressed before data import.

A few points to note on LEN.

This function counts the number of characters and returns the total number of characters for the following:

- text strings
- number data
- hyphens, ampersands, and per cent signs are examples of special characters.
- non - printing characters
- characters for space - including spaces between words

It only took a few clicks to do the task. All problem addresses are identified with an Excel text function.

The Difference Between An Excel Formula And An Excel Function

What is the distinction between a Formula and a Function? This is a topic I am asked a lot when it comes to Excel. I'll go over the differences and give some instances in this section.

A formula in Excel is a statement expressed by a spreadsheet user that requires computation to achieve a certain outcome. These formulae can be as straightforward or complicated as the user desires. Values, references to cells, specified names, and Functions may all be found in a Formula—but more on that later.

Let's get this party started. The equals = symbol must be at the beginning of a formula. If you don't enter this sign, Excel will treat your cell entries as text and won't calculate them.

So, following the equals sign, a formula will include the cell reference or address of the values to be modified or computed utilizing multiple operands in between.

In addition, Multiplication, Division, Subtraction, and Exponents are examples of common mathematical operators you are likely to be familiar with.

An example of a basic formula is =A1+B1, which is placed into cell A2 and represents the sum of two numbers.

The contents of cells A1 and B1 will be added, and the result will be shown in cell A2.

In summary, an Excel Formula is entered directly into the Formula bar; it lacks built-in wizards, cannot be nested, and is often a basic computation.

While an Excel Function is a collection of pre-programmed instructions executing an action and returning a value, a formula is not. Another way to put it is that a function is a formula in Excel that has already been developed for you. SUM, COUNT, IF, AVERAGE, and so on, for example.

What's wonderful about Functions that may be nested inside of each other is that they can be used to simplify difficult formulas. They include a built-in wizard to help the user through the various components of the function.

In the Formulas Tab, all of these pre-programmed functions are gathered together. To get to them, go to the Formulas Tab or click the insert function fx button to open the function dialogue box.

You may use a Function in three ways: start entering the operation you want to execute, such as SUM, AVERAGE, or choose the calculation category, such as Date & Time, Financial, or TEXT, and lastly, scroll through all of the available possibilities.

So, using the same example as before, a function that produces the same result and can be written as a formula is =SUM(A1:B1), which sums the contents of cells A1 and B1 and displays the contents of cell A2.

Is it possible to combine the two?

Yes, you can, and many people do so to make more difficult computations easier. Let's look at a couple of examples.

13. UNDERRATED MS EXCEL

Microsoft Excel should be used by anybody who wants to arrange any part of their life. Microsoft Excel is one of the most underappreciated computer programs. With the help of Microsoft Excel, everyone can make a difference in their lives.

To begin, when you open Microsoft Excel, you'll see that it comes with a variety of templates that you may use right away. Calendars, cash flow analyses, stock analyses, travel expense budgets, project to-do lists, inventory lists, and so on. Everything you'll need is right in front of you. Anyone might benefit from any or all of these. Microsoft Excel has tutorials on its home page, where you may choose your design. The lesson offers you a quick rundown of all they have to offer, but it doesn't show you everything they offer.

Excel is beneficial to any business owner for a variety of reasons. Businesses commonly use Excel for budgeting and monthly sales. Management usually inputs and tracks this data in a way that represents the company's foundation. Excel can make simple graphs out of this data to show employees how well or poorly they are doing. Not only that, but Excel arranges the data into tables that are simple to read for everyone. This is critical for company investors and stakeholders. When kids are continuously reading documents all day, having information that is so essential to them in the simplest of ways will make them extremely happy. Showing them their money and where it is going would also make them very happy. Excel may provide a more detailed breakdown of data if necessary.

Employee payouts and dividends, profit and loss statements, employee sale average, location sales for bigger firms, and other financial data are frequently kept in Excel by businesses. Excel provides excellent access to and simplicity of retrieval of this data. Anyone can examine a business folder, but there are instances where management is the only one who has access to this information.

Excel can import data, tables, computations, and other tasks into any other Microsoft template. This might be helpful when writing proposals. A graph or table may be exported into Microsoft Word to truly highlight what is attempting to be conveyed in a report. Also, Access is a wonderful tool for entering data and preserving it for later use, with Excel being used to export the data and build tables from it.

Excel can turn any business around. Excel has the power to transform any student or family. The simplicity with which information may be organized is remarkable. The simplicity with which knowledge may be accessed is astounding. The flow of using Excel is only made faster with the aid of the book and package described above. You may use basic to-do lists, simple budgets, simple calendars, and other tools if you don't have time to learn all the software's features. Any organization would be wise to learn about the entire range of benefits that this wonderful application, which is already installed on most PCs, has to offer. What matters is how simple it is. Excel is less difficult to learn than Access or other data input applications. In tiny businesses, it's essential to keep things simple.

Tips for Increasing Excel Calculation Speed

Normally, Excel updates its spreadsheets without your knowledge whenever you modify, even recalculating cells that haven't changed. When you have a workbook that has increased in size and is large enough to recalculate hundreds if not thousands of cells, it will freeze for a few moments while it updates.

There is no one-size-fits-all solution for speeding up computations in an Excel workbook, but here are a few recommendations that might assist.

1. Make a change to the way Excel calculates. Excel calculates automatically by default. You may set this to manual calculations so that it does not update when it isn't needed. Then select the "Calculation Options" option under the "Formulas" tab. Select "Manual" from the drop-down menu that displays. This will stop Excel from calculating cells until you press the "F9" key or select the "Calculate Now" button. You may now make changes to your spreadsheet without having to wait for Excel to finish calculating each time.

2. Combine all of your information onto a single worksheet. When Excel has to pull data from a separate sheet, it takes longer to calculate. This technique may not be practicable or appropriate if the data is on a different worksheet for design or access reasons.

3. Examine your spreadsheet for any formulae that include repetitive computations. If you have thousands of formulae in column "B" and they all include "($B$1+$C$1)" in their formula, Excel will do the calculation thousands of

times every time it calculates the worksheet. Replace that portion of your formula concerning a static cell in your workbook. Excel will only need to do the computation once, saving you significant calculation time.

4. Sort your data columns if possible. On sorted data, Excel functions execute considerably quicker. Select a column and then hit the "Sort and Filter" button under the "Home" tab to sort the column. "Sort A to Z" or "Sort Z to A" are the options.

5. If at all feasible, replace volatile functions with non-volatile ones. Volatile functions must be recalculated every time the worksheet is changed in any way. The seven volatile functions are RAND, NOW, TODAY, OFFSET, CELL, INDIRECT, and INFO. While avoiding them is not always practicable, try to use them as little as possible.

To assist you to speed up your Excel worksheet computations, use the five methods listed above.

14. MICROSOFT OFFICE 2021 WITH UPGRADED INTERFACE AND NEW DATA FEATURES

Microsoft Corp. has released some early details about the upcoming version of Office, which will have an improved user interface, new capabilities that allow users to handle data in Excel more freely, and other improvements.

The release, dubbed Office 2021, was unveiled on Thursday. It's not to be confused with Microsoft 365, the cloud-based version of the company's productivity package. They both feature the same basic apps; however, Office is a one-time purchase, whereas Microsoft 365 is a monthly subscription.

Office 2021 will enhance the performance of the suite's apps. There will also be new accessibility features and a dark option in Word, which Microsoft hasn't detailed yet. When users use Office on a laptop, the mode can save electricity and minimize screen glare in low-light situations. Microsoft hasn't revealed anything about the changes to other Office apps included in the update. However,

Microsoft told The Verge that Excel would get two new capabilities to simplify dealing with spreadsheets.

The first, known as dynamic arrays, will add to Excel's data-analytics capabilities. The spreadsheet editor contains a wide number of pre-made formulae that may be used to determine the average quarterly revenue for the last two years. The formula's output is often compressed into a single spreadsheet cell, which can cause formatting difficulties for sophisticated business computations with many outputs. To save time, dynamic arrays arrange findings into distinct cells automatically.

Excel will also get a feature called XLOOKUP from Microsoft, allowing users to look for data in a particular spreadsheet row rather than trawling through the whole spreadsheet. This is especially beneficial in complicated texts with a high number of identical components. A user can, for example, find the row holding the name of a vehicle part and then use XLOOKUP to rapidly go to the cell in the same row showing the item's price.

The most significant distinction between Office and Microsoft 365 is their intended purpose outside of the pricing plan. Employee devices that don't have consistent internet connectivity and can't use Microsoft 365's cloud capabilities are commonly used in the office.

Because of security concerns, a computer used to operate industrial equipment in a factory could run on an isolated network. Some businesses opt to acquire Office licenses as a one-time payment rather than subscribe to Microsoft 365.

Office 2021 will be accessible in a variety of formats. The versions aimed at consumers and small companies will cost the same as the current Office release, while those aimed at bigger corporations would cost 10% more.

Another change that may affect corporate customers is that Microsoft will support Office 2021 for five years rather than the customary seven years. Customers will have to upgrade sooner to continue receiving software updates. In a blog post, Microsoft 365 division corporate vice president Jared Spataro stated that the next edition of the suite would be released in the second half of 2022.

Excel 2021's Most Common and Useful Features

Data manipulation is made much easier with the help of Excel. Alternatively, information is important to the success of every organization. Alternatively, information is important to the success of every organization. You know how to operate or deal with any business if you know how to work with data. Numerous digital companies, such as Facebook, Google, and Microsoft, are dependent on data, and by analyzing data's behavior, they can generate large amounts of revenue with little effort. In this part, you'll discover some fundamental methods and tools for understanding and analyzing data that might help a novice. This section will be divided into three primary sections, each of which will have its subsections. So let's get this party started...

Section 1: Verifying the number of certain data points.

In Excel, there are three commonly used functions for counting any row or column.

- Make a tally (Start Address: End Address) The count of numerical numbers such as 1,2,3,4, 5,...1000 up to infinity is calculated using this function.
- A Count (Start Address: End Address) The user can use this function to count alphanumeric characters. It may be anything from A to Z, a to z, or 0–9 unique characters.
- CountBlank is a program that counts the number of blank spaces in (Start Address: End Address). This function

determines how many blank cells are available in a given column or row.

Let's look at how to use this feature.

Let's make some sample data to work with this function:

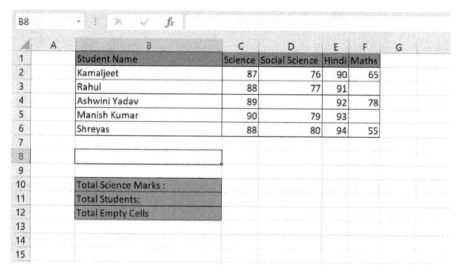

B8	∵	✕ ✓	f_x					
	A	B	C	D	E	F	G
1		Student Name	Science	Social Science	Hindi	Maths	
2		Kamaljeet	87	76	90	65	
3		Rahul	88	77	91		
4		Ashwini Yadav	89		92	78	
5		Manish Kumar	90	79	93		
6		Shreyas	88	80	94	55	
7							
8							
9							
10		Total Science Marks :					
11		Total Students:					
12		Total Empty Cells					
13							
14							
15							

Sample data to work with excel

Count() Function:

Let's calculate the total science marks using the count function because it can calculate the numerical values.

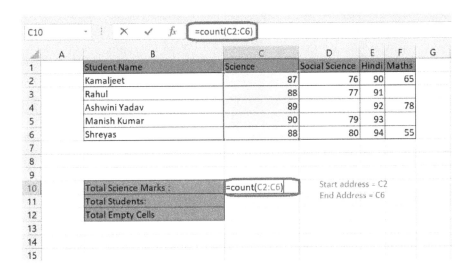

How can I use Excel's count function?

After using the formula: Count (Start Address: End Address) Function: 5, correct, we obtained the following output.

| C10 | | | ✗ | ✓ | f_x | =COUNT(C2:C6) | | | |

▲	A	B	C	D	E	F
1		Student Name	Science	Social Science	Hindi	Maths
2		Kamaljeet	87	76	90	65
3		Rahul	88	77	91	
4		Ashwini Yadav	89		92	78
5		Manish Kumar	90	79	93	
6		Shreyas	88	80	94	55
7						
8						
9						
10		Total Science Marks :	5			
11		Total Students:				
12		Total Empty Cells				
13						
14						
15						
16						
17						

CountA() Function

This is used to compute alphabetic data; therefore, let's figure out how many pupils are available.

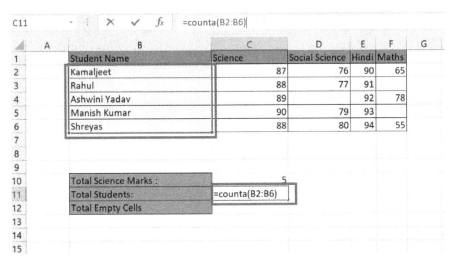

How to use CountA function

By applying the count() function using the same technique as we did for Count(). The only thing that changed here is the function name and address, which is B2:B6. The output comes as follows:

C11		fx	=COUNTA(B2:B6)			
	A	B	C	D	E	F
1		Student Name	Science	Social Science	Hindi	Maths
2		Kamaljeet	87	76	90	65
3		Rahul	88	77	91	
4		Ashwini Yadav	89		92	78
5		Manish Kumar	90	79	93	
6		Shreyas	88	80	94	55
7						
8						
9						
10		Total Science Marks :	5			
11		Total Students:	5			
12		Total Empty Cells				
13						
14						
15						

CountA CountBlank() Function Output

Because there are some empty numbers in the math column, let's compute them using the same approach. We must modify the name and address of the function for which we want to calculate the empty values.

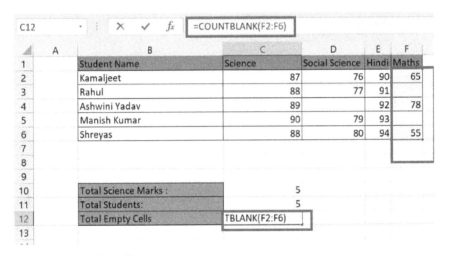

C12			✗ ✓ fx	=COUNTBLANK(F2:F6)			
	A	B		C	D	E	F
1		Student Name		Science	Social Science	Hindi	Maths
2		Kamaljeet		87	76	90	65
3		Rahul		88	77	91	
4		Ashwini Yadav		89		92	78
5		Manish Kumar		90	79	93	
6		Shreyas		88	80	94	55
7							
8							
9							
10		Total Science Marks :		5			
11		Total Students:		5			
12		Total Empty Cells		TBLANK(F2:F6)			
13							

Count blank function

The output of the blank count function will be as expected:

A	B	C	D	E	F	G
	Student Name	Science	Social Science	Hindi	Maths	
	Kamaljeet	87	76	90	65	
	Rahul	88	77	91		
	Ashwini Yadav	89		92	78	
	Manish Kumar	90	79	93		
	Shreyas	88	80	94	55	
	Total Science Marks :		5			
	Total Students:		5			
	Total Empty Cells		2			

The blank count function's output

Section 2: Validation of Data

We may utilize data validation if we don't want a user to add impure data into our excel sheet. There are several sorts of data validations accessible, including the following:

Types of Validation in Excel	Description
Whole Number	Takes input of whole numbers specified by the User
Decimal	Takes input of Decimal specified by the User
List	Creates a Dropdown list for specified values
Date	Takes input of Date Specified by user
Time	Takes Input of Time Specified by user
Text Length	Takes Input for specified text Length by User
Custom	Validates the data based on the formula put by user

Types of data validation in Excel

As an example, consider how to apply data validation.

A single number Validation of data: entire number The majority of data validation checks the data for the whole number.

Step 1: Select the column and move the pointer to data in the menu bar, as seen in the figure below.

Names	Roll No
Kamal	1201
Narayan	1202
Purnima	1203
Amit	1204
Shashank	1205
Manish	1206

Step 2: Select data validation as seen in the figure below.

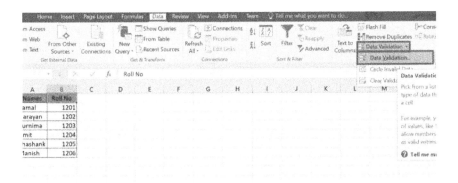

Excel Validation

Step 3: select entire in allow and enter the max and min values as shown in the figure below.

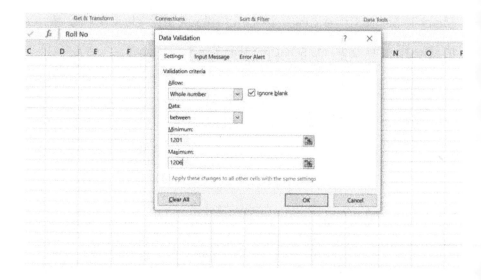

Step 4: After validation, if we enter a number outside the acceptable range, we will receive an issue, as seen in the image below.

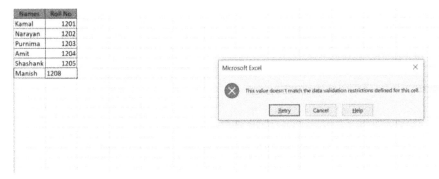

Excel mistake

Decimal Data Validation:

Decimal validation is primarily concerned with floating values.

Follow the steps above to get to the data validation dialog box, and then alter the validation as seen in the image below:

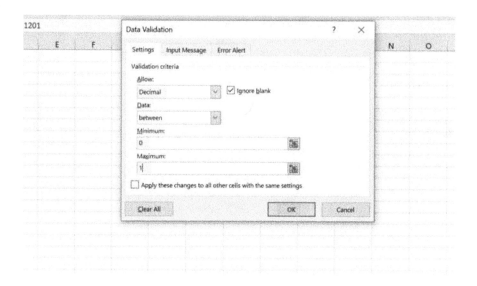

Then we may input any decimal number in our column and prevent any errors.

Validation of the list data:

Then, as seen in the following image, browse to the data validation dialog box and make changes to the validation settings:

Following the validation application, we can observe that a dropdown menu appears on the chosen cell.

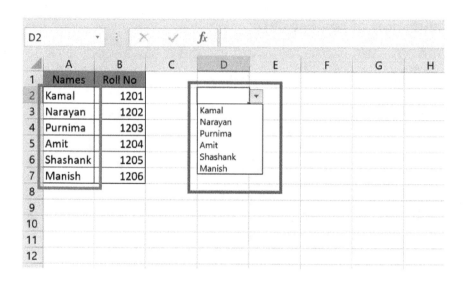

The message of Input/Error

To get to the data validation dialog box, follow the steps above and then alter the validation as shown below:

Message for Input:

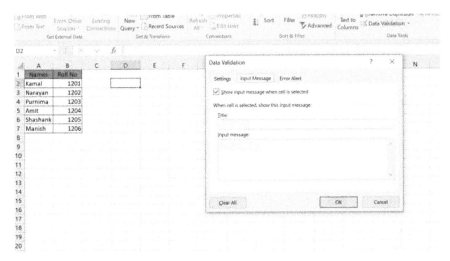

Input data validation

For error messages follow the below image:

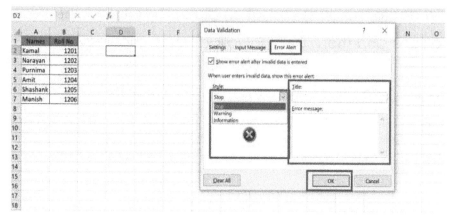

Error data validation

This is how we do validation, and we can try with some examples in the next blog.

These are the ways using that we can implement the functions in Excel. If, Countif, Countlfs, Sumlf, Sumlfs, Choose, and RandBetween are some of the functions that may be used for various reasons.

CONCLUSION

The entire purpose of Excel is to provide the greatest available assistance for a certain task, whether it is linked to education or business. Finance and accounting, particularly in business, cannot advance a single step without software. Product management and marketing must rely on forecasting based on Excel trend data. The possibilities are endless. Too many to list. For any business, it will always be the most helpful and adaptable piece of software. A firm employs Excel to excel in its endeavors, as its name suggests.

Excel is perhaps the most significant piece of computer software in today's industry. That is why so many employees and potential employees must learn Excel to enter or stay in the workforce.

The usage of Excel as an end-user computing tool is essential from the employer's perspective, especially those in the field of information systems. A growing number of companies use Excel for decision assistance, and numerous business professionals are utilizing it to conduct routine functional activities in the office.

Excel, in general, leads the spreadsheet product business, with an estimated market share of 90%. Excel 2007 can handle spreadsheets with up to a million rows and 16,000 columns, allowing users to import and manipulate large quantities of data and execute calculations quicker than ever before.

Excel is widely used for routine problem solving outside of the office.

Let's pretend you've got a home office. Excel can calculate sales tax, vehicle travel costs, temperature conversions, pizza prices per square inch, and data analysis. You may keep track of your debt, income, and assets, calculate your debt-to-income ratio and calculate your net worth, all of which can help you prepare for the process of applying for a new home loan. Excel has almost as many personal purposes as commercial ones, and an Excel lesson digs into the program's practical applications for both personal and corporate use.

Spreadsheets on computers are not a new concept. Spreadsheets have existed in electronic form since before the invention of the personal computer. Packages like VisiCalc, which were designed and patterned after an accountant's financial ledger, were forerunners of Excel and Lotus 1-2-3. Spreadsheet applications have influenced the corporate sector since 1987. Computerized spreadsheets have evolved into a ubiquitous and more effective tool for comparative data analysis worldwide.

End users now use Excel to generate and alter spreadsheets and author web pages with links and complicated formatting requirements. They create macros and scripts. While some of these programs are simple one-off computations, many are far more important and impact important financial choices and commercial transactions.

Many end-users and business experts rely on Microsoft Excel for their work. It is used by accountants and companies alike.

Excel's versatility allows it to be used as a receiver of workplace or company data, as well as a calculator, decision-making tool, data converter, and even a display spreadsheet for data interpretation. Excel can make a graph or chart, work with Mail Merge tools, import data from the Internet, build a concept map, and rank information in order of relevance.

Excel now includes additional data analysis and visualization features that make it easier to analyze data, detect patterns, and access data than ever before. With colored gradients, data bars, and icons, you may analyze and show significant trends and highlight exceptions using conditional formatting and rich data presentation methods.

Excel can be modified to handle a broad range of activities, and many organizations would not run without it. Many businesses now need Excel training; computer software training is a requirement for any company attempting to stay up with the trends.

Let's assume you have 97 employees, 17 of them have phoned in sick today, and you want to know what proportion of them are absent. That is something Excel is capable of. Excel can be used to determine the gender pay gap, the number of minorities on staff, and the amount of each employee's compensation package, including the percentages of income and benefits. You may use Excel to keep track of production by department, which can help you plan for future growth. You may use extra spreadsheets to keep track of data on vendors and customers while keeping track of product supply.

Let's assume you want to know how much your company produces vs. how much it costs. To use Excel, you don't need to be an expert in arithmetic; all you need is a fundamental grasp of the software. You may enter all of the data, analyze it, arrange it in your format, and display the findings using color, shading, backdrops, icons, and other gimmicks to make it simpler to find the data you need later. If you're making a presentation out of this spreadsheet, Excel can help you put it together in such a manner that the data seems to pop and glitter.

Learning Excel is one of the most significant things an employer can do; it is one of the most vital tools in the workplace.

Microsoft and Excel are registered trademarks of Microsoft Corporation in the United States and other countries.

ABOUT THE AUTHOR

Anthony Python was born in Chicago (USA). His passion for computers and programming began at a young age.

From the very beginning he showed interest in programming. He graduated in '04 from the University of Chicago with top marks in the *"Data Analyst"* degree course.

He says that he wants to transmit this skills to as many people as possible and in the easiest possible way.

CPSIA information can be obtained
at www.ICGtesting.com
Printed in the USA
LVHW020022160222
711186LV00003B/169